Day Trips with a Splash
Swimming Holes of the Southwest

by Pancho Doll

Running Water Publications
San Diego, California

Read this

Hiking is a potentially dangerous activity. Some sites in this book are reached via unmaintained trails or by overland travel where no trail may be present. As such, they require skill and strength beyond normal requirements for safe hiking. Although the book tries to point out potential dangers, conditions may change on the trail as well as in the water. River levels fluctuate widely during the year. Seasonal indicators are meant as guidelines, not as guarantees of when a place may be safe for swimming. People regularly drown or are seriously injured because they overestimate their abilities or exercise otherwise poor judgement. Rocks in rivers may be steep and slippery. Be cautious and aware even when walking casually in a river or creek bed. Jumping into water from rocks is inherently dangerous. You are responsible for locating submerged obstacles that could cause injury.

The overwhelming majority of swimming holes featured here are entirely on public land. A few cross, or lie near private land that, when visited for this book, did not appear to be posted or were marked with signs giving the public limited permission to use the property. In all events, you must obey no trespassing signs.

Library of Congress Cataloguing-in-Publication Data

Doll, Pancho

Day Trips with a Splash: Swimming Holes of the Southwest

Includes Index.

1. Hiking—Southwest—Guide-books.

2. Trails—Southwest—Guide-books.

ISBN 0-9657686-2-7   LCCN 99-091788

Acknowledgments

Thanks to my many friends and family for their support and encouragement, among them Paul Harton, Sean Haffey, Alan Hagman, Jeff MacDonald, Rodney Bosch and Vic Pappalardo. Special thanks go out to Will and Jennifer Daly in appreciation for their good cheer and hot water. And to Cheryl and Dexter Hewett. Thanks for editing to Jill Mahanna, who I promise that next time I'll read the Chicago Manual of Style *before* writing a book.

The Running Water Staff

Photographer	Duncan Freely
Diving Consultant	Flip Obermore
Spiritual Advisor	Rev. Bob Tism
Wardrobe	Ngo Tan Ligne
Hydrologist	Flo Engover

To my mom for being ever willing to load us
kids in the car and take us to the river.

You could tell by the dent of the heel and the sole
They was lots o' fun on hand at the old swimmin' hole

— James Whitcomb Riley (1849-1916)

Contents

Tucson & the Chiricahuas

Phoenix Area

The Mogollon Rim

Introduction

Try this. Make an appointment with your banker. Explain that you want a business loan to open a chain of lingerie shops in fundamentalist Moslem countries or to sell beach chairs in the High Arctic. The reaction you get will be similar to puzzled expression friends and family made when I announced plans to write a book about swimming holes in the desert.

I wasn't really sure whether to take myself seriously either, so I picked April 1 as the date to start the research and the Santa Catalina Mountains in Tucson as the place.

Contrary to apprehensions, when I asked about swimming holes, enthusiastic volunteers pointed me up what seemed like every canyon. Most of the time they were right.

It began a season of discovery. Plunge pools scuba deep and great slabs of sandstone form smooth containers of cool water. In the Southwest a person can enjoy an intimate tub deeply shaded by sycamore or the Gothic shock of tall rock stretching ¼-mile along deep water.

Many places featured here are so little visited that they don't have agreed-upon names. In most cases, the names I selected are based on the canyon the hole is in, the trail it's along, or natural features nearby. Where there are more than a couple of holes on the same stretch of water, I made up the name myself.

All of them are lovingly recorded in a collection of photos painted in the primary colors of the Southwest: blue sky, red rock and green water.

I also gathered some interesting geologic samples. I had little spheres of sandstone called Navajo marbles that I picked up near Lake Powell and some geodes I found up near Zane Grey's cabin in Payson, Arizona. The collection rode along unobtrusively for 20,000 miles, all held in place by camera bags, climbing equipment and so forth... all until I got home.

Too tired to unpack, I flopped on the bed, pleased and maybe even a little smug about my success with such an unlikely topic. While I enjoyed a self-satisfied rest inside, thieves jimmied the driver side door. I didn't discover the theft until the first stop sign the next morning when I heard the stones roll forward and crash against the cargo box in the back of the truck.

The first thing I looked for were the photos. Still there. But the thieves inadvertently grabbed a bag containing the microcassettes I used to record field notes. They amounted to six months of research without which I could not write the book.

I cleared my schedule for the next summer and prepared for the Zen exercise of paying twice for the same real estate.

While not strictly speaking a spiritual experience, the act of reliving a portion of one's life delivered some fascinating symmetry. Fifty three weeks later, on the last day of the desert redux, my truck got burglarized *again*.

It was at a canyon I'd failed to find twice before. But, since swimming hole scholarship doesn't favor slackers, I made a last attempt and was rewarded with four magnificent places that I photographed before turning back toward the research vessel where I would drink a beer then drive west toward my reward. Just a few steps remaining.

But what's this? The cooler was missing. Other stuff, too. *Again.*

After some time gesturing wildly with a pistol, I decided the only remedy was a search for meaning.

It might be a straight up Sunday school story about pride prefiguring the fall. Perhaps it was some karmic debt repaid with double compounded interest or simply the cruel teeth of a meaningless universe.

Experience favored the latter. In becoming a swimming hole professional, I learned that goalposts keep moving. The physical objective is always deeper down the canyon or higher up the watershed, farther along the road and closer to the middle of nowhere.

The burglaries only showed that an object, once collected, resists possession and the purpose to which it's dedicated evades completion. Gravity is real; rocks are hard. Disorder is the rule and entropy always wins.

I still lock doors and back up data, but the most durable defense is to accept reward in the activity itself.

By that measure the loss of property and the expense of 40,000 miles felt good. It felt really good. It felt like finding water in the desert.

Using this guide

The convention in outdoor guide books is to take a small area and detail *every* trail in it. This book takes a region and, using swimming holes as a theme, tells readers the *best* places to go. Beyond a unique subject matter, *Day Trips with a Splash* is laid out in a new, easy-to-use format. One page is a USGS topographic map with directions and latitude/longitude coordinates for those with global positioning system (GPS) receivers. The facing page has a picture of the swimming hole along with the review and icons detailing key information about the spot.

I tried to include a range of difficulties in each chapter, some accessible enough to take small children, others remote and with a high expectation of privacy. But first, a few terms need to be outlined in a quick and dirty glossary so you know what you're getting into.

Moderate scrambling means you might bash a knee or skin an elbow and your friends may laugh at you.

Third-class scrambling means that if you fall, it will hurt. You may receive injuries and your friends might have to help you back to the car. You may even need medical help.

Bushwacking is considered light if you can do it in shorts. It's moderate if you wish you had pants on. It's heavy if you wish you had pants and boots.

Basins are broad and shallow, usually less than four feet deep. Little or no sense of enclosure.

Pools are deeper, between six and eight feet deep with proportionately less surface area than basins.

Tubs have an even smaller surface area, usually room for only a couple of people. They're five to seven feet deep with near complete enclosure and are most often associated with waterfalls.

Holes are generally the same proportion as a pool but deeper and with a tighter enclosure. If you can dive into it, it's a hole.

The Approach

The right-most icon tells how long or difficult the hike is. Most people are familiar with the symbols ski areas use to evaluate the difficulty of the slopes. Here they are redefined for hiking.

 Beginner Less than one-half hour. No more than a couple of tricky steps. You can bring kids.

 Intermediate Up to one hour. May include moderate scrambling, boulder hopping, bush-whacking or amphibious hiking. You feel like a kid.

 Advanced Longer and/or steeper approach. May include extensive boulder hopping, deep river fords or 3rd class scrambling with potentially injurious fall. Leave the kids at home.

 Expert Three-hour approaches over difficult terrain or technical approaches requiring rope. No kidding around.

The Season

The set of icons to the left of the approach icons tells you which season is best for each swimming hole. Remember, conditions vary and there's no reliable way to look at a calendar and judge when a river is safe.

In addition, the summer monsoon season produces isolated thunder showers. These, combined with poor soil permeability and steep, narrow canyons, mean that a wall of water can unexpectedly roar down a canyon, returning you and your friends to the nutrient chain sooner than you would like.

To avoid this result, always check weather before embarking. Ensure that high pressure dominates, both in the area you want to visit and the area upstream.

Spring Smaller or dryer watersheds. The spring swimming holes open as soon as the water's warm enough (April or so) and end when the water gets stagnant. The closing varies greatly, but the fourth of July is a good benchmark.

 Summer Fourth of July through Labor Day. Usually streams and creeks between 1,500 and 4,000 feet elevation. Some are better earlier in the summer, some later. If the hole has both a spring and a summer designation that means late June through July is best.

 Fall As late as October at lower elevations. Some steep, narrow swimming holes on smaller streams may receive a fall designation because water is too fast even during the moderate summer flow. A summer and a fall combination means water may still be too high in early July and you might have to wait until later in the month.

The Company

The next group contains four icons which generally let you know who or what you can bring for companionship and who you're likely to find.

 Kids You're generally safe bringing little dippers of any age to a swimming hole with a beginner's approach. However, short approach holes without a child icon indicates either the rocks are too steep or the water is otherwise inappropriate for junior. On an intermediate approach, a child under seven may tire.

Dogs Many dog owners have difficulty finding places to take their canine pals, what with restrictions on dogs in wilderness areas and national parks. The "Bowser" icon indicates spots in national forests where you don't *have* to keep the dog on a leash and where he's not going to run into lots of other hikers and disturb them. Also where the terrain is appropriate.

 The Boom Box Brigades Crowds likely. Potentially rowdy. Likely to be evidence of at least one broken beer bottle.

 The Butt indicates one of two things. Either there's a chance you will find skinny dippers or the place is private enough that you and your companion(s) can opt for no tan lines.

Overall rating

The left-most icon is the overall rating. There are about a dozen points on which to judge the quality of a particular spot. The Holy Trinity is height, depth and privacy. The ratings are fair, good, excellent and classic.

To get an excellent rating they must have some compelling vertical feature like a fall or a jumping rock. A swimming hole may not be rated classic and also have a boom box designation.

The privacy assessment is based on what you'd expect to find during a peak weekend. Most of the spots are far enough up canyon that if you do meet other people, they're apt to be like-minded outdoors enthusiasts who will enhance the experience rather than detract from it.

Doubtful means one dozen or more people in the area. Bring a bag to pick up trash other people leave behind.

Possible indicates fewer than six people likely. Consider going elsewhere on weekends.

Likely suggests the most you would expect to find is one other group.

Guaranteed says little evidence of visitorship other than a slight trail. If somebody else arrives at the swimming hole, you're probably being followed.

Usability

Usability is the collection of features that make a swimming hole comfortable for humans. It's difficult to take full enjoyment of a spot if it's too steep to sit down. Bare rock and blazing sun can shorten a day, too.

Seating A well-shaded sand beach is best. Low angle slabs can be very comfortable, especially if the rock has smooth declivities worn in it by the water. These depressions are called *buckets* if they're just big enough for only one to sit in. Seating for two or more is called a *bench seat*. A slab is considered flat if a can rolls slowly enough that you can catch it before it hits the water. It's sloping if you can't set the can upright without it tipping over. The slab is considered steep if there's a danger you yourself might tip over. Boulders are less comfortable than slabs. Typically they're more jagged and many are too small to lie on at all. For the purposes of this book, boulders are considered small if they're the size of a trunk. Medium boulders are the size of a car. Large boulders are the size of a cabin and massive boulders are the size of a house.

Sun and shade On what part of the swimming hole will the sun be shining from mid-afternoon on and is there a place you can go to escape it.

Entry and Exit There are more than a few swimming holes you can jump in only to realize there's no easy way back out.

Temperature Water in the mid 60 to 70 degrees is considered just about ideal.

Jumps Basically how high. Where possible I've tried to explain what the bottom features are like. Talk to locals if they're available for safety information, but most importantly get in the water and have a look around for yourself.

You are responsible for your own safety. Anyone jumping from cliffs should not depend solely on this guide for safety information.

Aesthetics

This is another qualitative category describing the water and the shape of the rock enclosure.

Water quality Mainly the clarity and color of the water, whether gin clear, Coke-bottle green, emerald, jade, turquoise or tea. What's the visibility and does it have much plant glop. Points are deducted if there's a dam upstream. Human pollution is largely irrelevant since nearly all the spots are on national forest land and well above any settlement, although range cattle lower water quality in a few places.

Geometric sides are either generally round or with coherent angles such that the waterline forms a recognizable shape like a rectangle or circle. The bottom is even, containing small cobbles, sand or smooth stone.

Wavy enclosures signify that straight lines or curves, when found, are not sustained. Submerged rocks and boulders may obscure the bottom contour.

Jagged swimming holes have no discernible lines to the rock structure. Not necessarily a bad thing. An apparent imperfection can become an attractive feature such as when large boulders poke through the surface to create platforms for diving or lounging.

The Maps

Material for the map pages was scanned from United States Geological Survey 7.5-minute topographic maps. In all but a few cases the elevation contours are 40 feet. Every effort was made to get the most current maps; however, trails are often not shown and some other information may be out of date. Although it's difficult to get completely lost following a stream or river, it's a good idea to bring a compass on long trips and be proficient in its use.

Where helpful, latitude and longitude annotations were added. Coordinates were checked against physical maps using the WGS 84 map datum. Pinpoint accuracy is what the GPS promises and usually delivers. Still, the possibility for error is significant, both in the operation of individual navigation units and in generating coordinates published here. The coordinates and the map location represent a best effort to locate the swimming hole being reviewed, but neither are guaranteed to be completely accurate.

Computer users can get electronic copies of the maps. Mail in a copy of the store reciept and follow registration instructions on the web site. Then download the maps to print out at home, much more elegant than taking the entire book into the hills when you only need two pages.

Finally, it's recommended that you use a forest service recreation map for highway information and for information on campgrounds if you want to make a car camping weekend of it.

Tactics and Ethics

The simple fact you're holding this book identifies you as a person of distinction and judgment. You're probably aware of low-impact outdoor ethics, don't cut switchbacks, that sort of stuff. Nevertheless, here are a couple things day users should keep in mind.

Don't urinate within 200 feet of open water. For solid waste dig a hole 6 inches deep and in soil exposed to sunlight.

Do not trample grass or vegetation in streambeds. It accounts for a tiny percentage of the regional habitat, but an overwhelming number of species rely on riparian areas for food, shelter and reproduction. Groups should be fewer than six individuals to avoid unintentional damage.

When hiking off trail don't skid down steep slopes. Rather, place your foot carefully and weight it gingerly so as not to dislodge dirt and rocks. A stealthy tread prevents erosion and avoids twisted ankles. In some cases where there is a steep descent or a stream crossing, it's an excellent idea to bring a ski pole or some sort of sturdy walking stick.

When walking on or near the stream, it's best to step on the tops of exposed rocks where possible. Avoid sloshing through shallow gravel and the stream margins. Lots of critters lay their eggs there and you can do a devil of a lot of damage with one footstep.

Cryptobiotic soil is the black crust that forms in the desert. It prevents erosion and the microbes therein fix nitrogen, a process critical to plants. It takes years to form, so stay on established trails. Where no trail is present walk footstep to footstep.

Don't damage Indian artifacts. Don't touch rock art and view ruins from a distance. These might seem like extreme measures, but archeologists are uniformly alarmed at the sudden degradation of these sites. We're loving them to death.

If you want to be a good steward of the outdoors, also bring an empty plastic bag big enough to hold a couple of beer cans or whatever other small bits of trash you may encounter.

Most of the approaches are best done in trail running shoes. Sports sandals are acceptable for the shorter and intermediate ones. Only a few require boots. Remember, he who is shod lightest travels fastest.

Tucson & the Chiricahuas

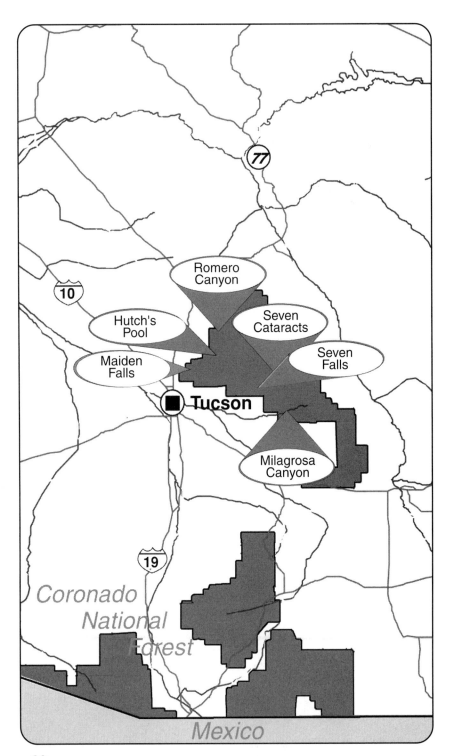

Romero Canyon

Seven Cataracts

Hutch's Pool

Seven Falls

Maiden Falls

Tucson

Milagrosa Canyon

Coronado National Forest

Mexico

10

77

19

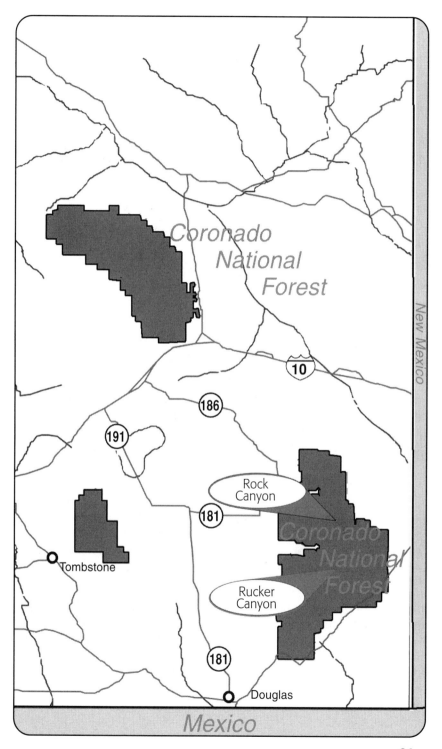

Coronado National Forest

New Mexico

10

186

191

Rock Canyon

181

Coronado National Forest

Tombstone

Rucker Canyon

181

Douglas

Mexico

Odometer Zero

Day One of the Southwest swimming hole project and I was going into the field with full canyoneering gear, rope, helmet, split-toe neoprene booties: everything.

I was crouched in the back of the Research Vessel digging for my telescoping aluminum trekking pole. I found it, but when I crawled to the tailgate, planted it on the ground and leaned on it, the thing collapsed. I tumbled and landed tenderloin first, smack on my mountain bike. The handlebar got me square in the left kidney.

Worse, there was a witness and she was attractive. I had to pretend like I meant to do it.

The elaborate preparations seemed appropriate since stream crossings, normally dry and sandy, were hip-deep with running water. Water was so high that one local told me alligators had been getting into people's backyards.

Alligators aside, my introduction to the desert ecosystem proceeded briskly, beginning with the plant life.

Among the cactus, "jumping cholla" has the worst reputation because its ability to find a passing victim suggests projectile capability. But in my experience plants of the agave family are the main culprits. It seemed that everywhere I wanted to go was guarded by a cluster of sharp, dagger shaped leaves. During three days I acquired more than 20 cuts and abrasions one inch or longer. A look at my arms and you'd think that I sort cats for a living.

Rocks were next. Geologists call this the Basin and Range Province, small mountain ranges like the Santa Catalinas, Peloncillos and Dragoon mountains, separated by flat desert. Native Americans call the mountains "sky islands" and that's how they'd look at night when I'd drive across a basin to the next morning's prospects.

Cattle outnumber people in this part of the state where vast horizons of desert scrub are punctuated with the occasional windmill and accompanying stock tank. Left turns are never a problem and if you break down, you needn't bother to turn on the hazards. I know this because of two flat tires and a dead battery. Here are a few other guidelines for driving in the Southwest.

The Steering Wheel Wave — Most important is when to wave. You should wave to the driver of an oncoming vehicle if:

- You are more than seven miles from a paved road. This, because dirt roads create a community of users, a rugged group of like-minded people who didn't accidentally turn off of the pavement.

- You are on a two-lane paved road and have seen fewer than three vehicles in more than 10 miles.

- You notice similar equipment, whether kayak, mountain bike or climbing stickers.

- You are out of gasoline.

Road Kill — Most vehicle-vs.-animal incidents happen at night, especially those involving domestic cats, although other species are involved.

- Rodents only count if you're driving on a learner's permit.

- You can identify rabbit species this way. Jackrabbits bounce up and hit the undercarriage; cottontails don't, unless you're driving too fast.

- Snakes are often difficult to find after they've been struck. Use the rearview mirror to spot them immediately after contact. Then season with garlic and lemon.

Directions — Most destinations in this book are saved as precise coordinates for GPS users. However, you might need some help interpreting supplementary information gained from locals.

- When discussing conditions on marginal dirt roads, ask respondent if they pay retail for their tires.

- Always ask for elevations when someone says, "it's over the hill."

- Randomly test respondent's knowledge of local geography by slowing to a stop, rolling down the window and asking simply, "how far is it?"

- Never ask respondent if they owned a cat. (see above)

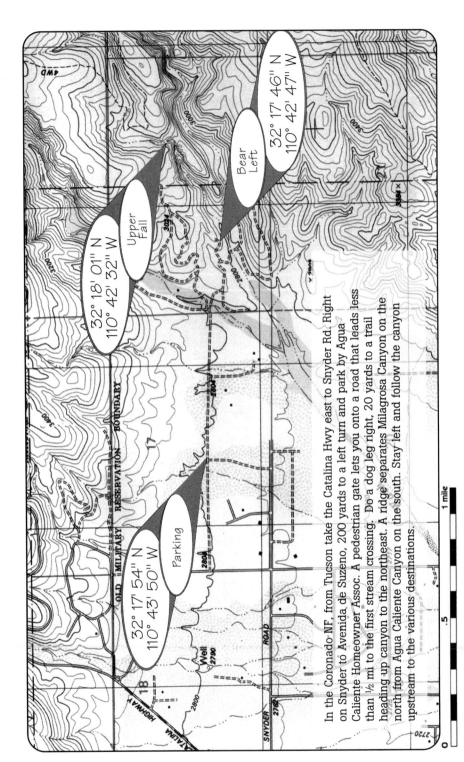

In the Coronado NF, from Tucson take the Catalina Hwy east to Snyder Rd. Right on Snyder to Avenida de Suzeno, 200 yards to a left turn and park by Agua Caliente Homeowner Assoc. A pedestrian gate lets you onto a road that leads less than ½ mi to the first stream crossing. Do a dog leg right, 20 yards to a trail heading up canyon to the northeast. A ridge separates Milagrosa Canyon on the north from Agua Caliente Canyon on the south. Stay left and follow the canyon upstream to the various destinations.

Parking
32° 17' 54" N
110° 43' 50" W

Upper Fall
32° 18' 01" N
110° 42' 32" W

Bear Left
32° 17' 46" N
110° 42' 47" W

Milagrosa Canyon

Bigger than Texas and with lots more depth. Pools are well shaded and apparently perennial. There are three of them separated by about 300 feet of elevation. The lower pool is an oval 25 feet on the major axis. On the right is a sand beach about 100 square feet. Nice ledges but none good enough for reclining. The left ledge is 45 feet high while another wall rises 200 feet. Diving is limited by rocks that overhang the water, so there's a substantial risk of clipping one on the way down, even though the water is plenty deep to stop a falling body.

The depth of the lower pool is a function of the middle pool which catches lots of the sand and gravel. So this middle pool is not as deep, but has really good sand pockets with cottonwoods as well as a ledge 10 feet wide with virtually unlimited seating. The upper fall is the real prize. It comes down a tube carved into the rock and cores out a tank of water about 35 feet long and 25 feet wide. Jumps are many. It's easy in and easy out via a rock collar with a sandy fringe.

You'll likely find 10 to 20 people on the weekend, but that number is easily accommodated by the three falls. Milagrosa Canyon is a classic by any measure.

Bonus Feature: You pass a popular sport climbing spot on the way. Difficulty ranges from 5.8 to 5.11b.

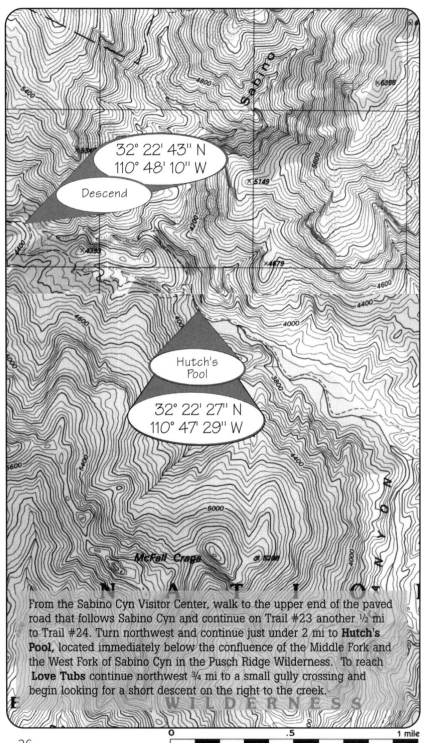

32° 22' 43" N
110° 48' 10" W

Descend

Hutch's
Pool

32° 22' 27" N
110° 47' 29" W

From the Sabino Cyn Visitor Center, walk to the upper end of the paved road that follows Sabino Cyn and continue on Trail #23 another ½ mi to Trail #24. Turn northwest and continue just under 2 mi to **Hutch's Pool,** located immediately below the confluence of the Middle Fork and the West Fork of Sabino Cyn in the Pusch Ridge Wilderness. To reach **Love Tubs** continue northwest ¾ mi to a small gully crossing and begin looking for a short descent on the right to the creek.

0   .5   1 mile

Love Tubs

The place to take a date. Blocky rocks create a modest buffet of four or so small tubs. They're nothing grand, but they do make a good place to get in and be cozy. Descending from the trail you come out onto a ledge paralleling the creek at about 50 vertical feet above the tubs. Best advice is to walk along the ledge to survey the prospects, then descend to the one that suits you. That said, the best one is at a tributary where a nicely formed tub, five to six feet deep is fed by a three-foot fall. There's good seating on some of the blocks. You can also plunk it down under a couple of small oaks, but no place really sensuous to lie down in the shade with a love interest.

Many of the boulders blocking the stream are due in part to an earthquake in 1885. It was centered in Mexico, but Tucson residents reported seeing dust rising from the Catalinas. However, geologists say many boulders in the canyon were there a long time before the quake.

The expectation of privacy is excellent, although the place isn't unknown. There's a cairn by the best tub. No descending trail, so there's a bit of bushwhacking involved, but you can weave your way among the sticky prickles. On the tributary stream are another couple of small tubs at the bottom of a twelve-foot cascade. Note that all these features are high in the watershed and apt to get green and slimy earlier in the season.

Milagrosa Canyon

Hutch's Pool

Greatly loved by rock jumpers. The tank is 80 feet long and 20 feet wide. Walls on each side range from 10 to 25 feet high. The lounging area is commodious with enough sand to park a semi on. Good thing too. The expectation of privacy is only fair, even on a weekday. There was not a scrap of litter when I visited because dutiful volunteers keep the trails clean in this heavily-used wilderness.

No more than 150 yards above there's a pleasant upstream escape from the one dozen people you might find on a weekend at Hutch's Pool. It's a miniature of Hutch's and surprisingly little visited. It would be killer except for three fallen boulders that really reduce the size of the sweet spot. Ledges are fractured and bumpy and there's not lots of shade. However, there is water all over the place, including three more small pools on the main canyon and a nice fall on the adjoining stream to the south.

What's more, about one quarter mile *below* Hutch, you'll pass a large outcrop about 80 feet high. Adjoining the outcrop is a basin 50 to 60 feet long. The top is filled with some short cascades. The best feature is a couple of deeply shaded lounging rocks. The deepest spot is a small tub at the top—enough to get in and splash around, but that's about it. Worth a pause, but not a destination in itself.

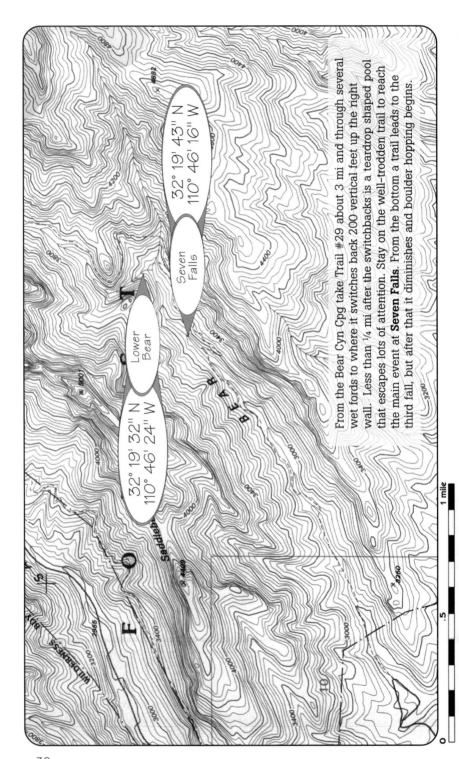

From the Bear Cyn Cpg take Trail #29 about 3 mi and through several wet fords to where it switches back 200 vertical feet up the right wall. Less than 1/4 mi after the switchbacks is a teardrop shaped pool that escapes lots of attention. Stay on the well-trodden trail to reach the main event at **Seven Falls**. From the bottom a trail leads to the third fall, but after that it diminishes and boulder hopping begins.

Lower Bear

32° 19' 32" N
110° 46' 24" W

Seven Falls

32° 19' 43" N
110° 46' 16" W

1 mile

.5

0

Lower Bear

Water can go from a roar to a whisper and color can range from dark, tannic red early in the season to a photosynthetic green after a month of low flow and steady sun. Also, the canyon has fascinating metamorphic rock that's been heated and twisted like hot taffy.

The most popular hole (apart from Seven Falls) is the lowest one where the canyon drains from the northeast. It has broad slabs that are oriented in the direction of the water's flow, creating smooth, low-angle seating, some that can accommodate lots of people. An awesome place to test new sunscreen. Shade? Forget it.

A little over 150 yards above is a teardrop-shaped pool about 35-feet across on the fat end. Small seating ledges are on the right, but they're a little rough on the user's bottom. Above is another pool, good to excellent. It's most notable for the shade created by a pair of sycamores that have bravely situated themselves in the middle of the stream where the water falls six vertical feet on either side. And there they stand, the two trees with a good amount of root structure exposed, but looking quite satisfied with their location. One of them even appears to be smiling.

Seven Falls

You have to do a whole lot of hiking before you'll find a place more beautiful than Bear Canyon and Seven Falls. The highest pool is bodacious, but they're steep with little place to sit. The second is a plunge pool at the bottom of a 100-foot fall. It just goes down and down. Gorgeous feature, but not a practical swimming hole. The third fall only has room for three to four people.

The fourth fall is 45 feet high and it creates a plunge pool surrounded by a lonely expanse of marble-smooth rock. There are beautifully sculpted butt buckets for backsides of any dimension, although the likelihood is that only those with slim athletic hips are likely to make it up here.

Most people collect at the fifth and sixth fall where there's a triangular pool that measures 80 feet at the hem. Slabs are big enough to hold a fraternity party. Visitorship is very high, but people don't seem to stay for too long. Part of the reason for the high turnover is that the south-facing canyon gets broiling. You might want to retreat to the shade down canyon. One other negative, the water contains lots of tannic acid. It's harmless, but it gives the water a reddish-brown color.

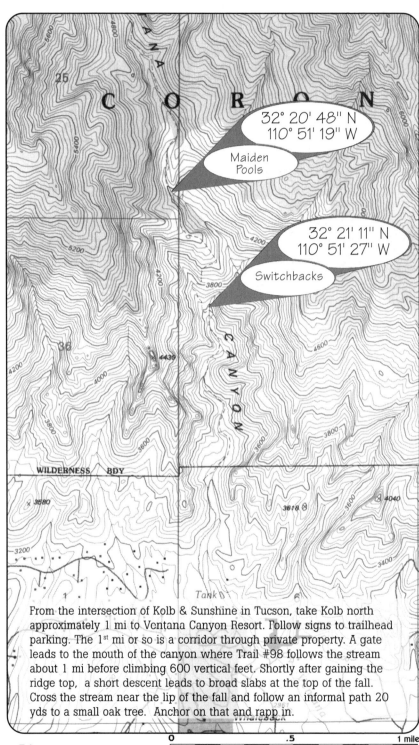

32° 20' 48" N
110° 51' 19" W

Maiden Pools

32° 21' 11" N
110° 51' 27" W

Switchbacks

From the intersection of Kolb & Sunshine in Tucson, take Kolb north approximately 1 mi to Ventana Canyon Resort. Follow signs to trailhead parking. The 1st mi or so is a corridor through private property. A gate leads to the mouth of the canyon where Trail #98 follows the stream about 1 mi before climbing 600 vertical feet. Shortly after gaining the ridge top, a short descent leads to broad slabs at the top of the fall. Cross the stream near the lip of the fall and follow an informal path 20 yds to a small oak tree. Anchor on that and rapp in.

Maiden Falls

Like having a backstage pass. If you know how to descend the fall, you can walk right past the 30 or more weekend visitors you're likely to find at Maiden Pools and pop right into a private spot less than 50 yards from the *hoi polloi*. Steep slabs hide it from view, so surprisingly few of the many visitors even know about it.

The fall is beautifully formed top to bottom. At the top, water exiting Maiden Pools accelerates into a long, slender rock chute, corkscrewing 40 feet through gneiss before plunging 90 vertical feet into an exquisite tub below. The tub is carved into more gneiss, a metamorphic formation characterized by bands of dark rock blended with lighter colored quartz. The bottom of the tub and surrounding walls appear meticulously inlaid by a stone mason of the abstract impressionist school.

A larger pool immediately downstream will be around six feet deep at the start of the season. It's bounded by brush, boulders and a tiny sand beach with shade from an oak tree. Broad slabs higher up to the right of the fall have enough room for all your friends, but unlike the visitorship at Maiden Pools, the bottom of the fall has guaranteed privacy. That's because you need a rope to get in. It's a pretty straight forward rappel. Even though it looks from the top as if you'd need more than 60-meter rope to reach the bottom, a standard length is plenty. Bring ascenders for an easy climb back out.

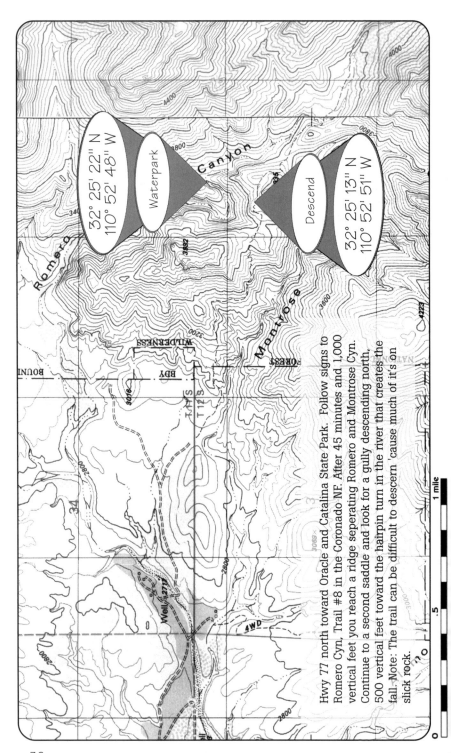

32° 25' 22" N
110° 52' 48" W

Waterpark

Descend

32° 25' 13" N
110° 52' 51" W

Hwy 77 north toward Oracle and Catalina State Park. Follow signs to Romero Cyn, Trail #8 in the Coronado NF. After 45 minutes and 1,000 vertical feet you reach a ridge seperating Romero and Montrose Cyn. Continue to a second saddle and look for a gully descending north, 500 vertical feet toward the hairpin turn in the river that creates the fall. Note: The trail can be difficult to descern 'cause much of it's on slick rock.

0   .5   1 mile

Romero Canyon

No, not the Romero everybody knows about. This is a place where a rock finger forces a hairpin turn in the creek, creating in the process four pools that amount to a water park better than Disney could build. Balanced rocks on the canyon wall to the right add to the scenery, while stone at the top of the fall is so beautifully milled by the water that golden light from the setting sun makes it appear like smooth butter.

The biggest fall is a two-step cascade, 60 feet high or so. Water comes down in three chutes. The left one runs hardest, but the right one falls into its own little cove. Very pretty and intimate. Down lower there's a short fall formed by a large boulder fallen into the rifle notch canyon. Below that there's a narrow slot pool 9 feet wide and 50 feet long. The boulder might present a dive platform, but swim around and check it out first. Farther down, on the other side of the rock finger, the river heads north out of the canyon.

In sum, a glorious place to sun and draw the envy of the other hikers looking down at the fall as they schlep along the trail to spend the afternoon with dozens of others at Romero Pools. It's not unvisited, though. An old fire ring indicates use. If you make it there, use care walking on delicate grass at the fringes of the pools. To avoid destroying the vegetation completely, enter and exit at the same place. Don't trample through the grass and mud.

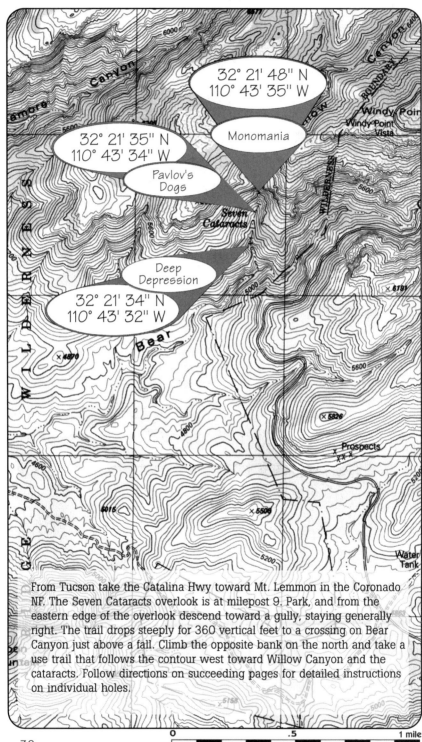

32° 21' 48" N
110° 43' 35" W

Monomania

32° 21' 35" N
110° 43' 34" W

Pavlov's Dogs

Deep Depression

32° 21' 34" N
110° 43' 32" W

Seven Cataracts

Windy Point
Windy Point Vista

From Tucson take the Catalina Hwy toward Mt. Lemmon in the Coronado NF. The Seven Cataracts overlook is at milepost 9. Park, and from the eastern edge of the overlook descend toward a gully, staying generally right. The trail drops steeply for 360 vertical feet to a crossing on Bear Canyon just above a fall. Climb the opposite bank on the north and take a use trail that follows the contour west toward Willow Canyon and the cataracts. Follow directions on succeeding pages for detailed instructions on individual holes.

0   .5   1 mile

Deep Depression

A little pool that's located so deep in the canyon, you have to order out for sunshine. The swimming hole is really no more than a bucket, five feet deep and about ten-feet wide. There are some ledges to sit on, but none larger than a single bed. There's nary a footprint here, although the hand of man is upon this place. Expect to find a few items of litter that wash down from Mt. Lemmon and the highway.

Privacy is excellent to guaranteed. This, because the approach is difficult. In fact, this swimming hole and two more reviewed on the following pages appear absolutely inaccessible. Thousands view them from the road, but located as they are on the far side of what appears to be a canyon with near vertical walls, they seem like some distant ivory tower. They are not. Follow the instructions on the map page until you get to the main canyon. To reach this hole turn downstream on the eastern bank a short distance or until you get to the water, then turn upstream to the pool.

The greatest danger on this approach is loose rock. Try to step only on larger rocks. Always have three points of contact: hand on walking stick, another hand on a piece of rock and another foot firmly placed before you load the other foot. Be especially careful of stones that appear flat. They are the ones most likely to slide.

Upper Pavlov's

Pavlov's Dogs

You'll salivate, too. These are a couple of holes close together. The lower fall (*pictured above*) is about 30 feet high and it fills a pool of about that width. Plenty of shade from a couple of pretty cedars and willows, plus a nice lounging rock on left side that's close to 40 square feet and situated right under a big, mature cedar. A diving rock 10 feet high adjoins the lounging slab and stands right over the fat end of the hole.

Upper Pavlov(*left*) is even better. A fall about 45 feet high cascades into a hole that would retain water even if it didn't rain until the next ice age. It's shaped like an isosceles triangle, 25 feet from the apex to the base and 45 feet wide at the base. Ample lounging rocks on both sides are deeply shaded. The only negative is that sloping sides of the hole itself don't offer any really good platforms from which to launch. Best jumping is at the lower pool.

The upper hole is reached by scrambling up a gully to the left of the first hole. Very loose rock and a steep angle. Continue bushwhacking to the left, switching back and forth on narrow, crumbly ledges. You'll gain a ledge with a faint trail that leads to the right and delivers you to the second hole. Also, visit a small fall just above the upper hole where a pair of large boulders pinch the water, causing it to hollow out a six-foot deep tub.

Monomania

How much will you pay for privacy? This is the pour-off, the top of the tumble, the high point where water from Mt. Lemmon begins its acceleration toward Tucson. Here, water has cored what looks like an elevator shaft deep down into the rock. The water falls close to 100 vertical feet into a pool that's ten feet wide, but less than six feet deep. The view is expansive, well above the road that's visible to the southwest.

To reach it, follow directions to Pavlov's. From the upper hole contour along the plateau, follow a faint trail that will deliver you to yet another fall, this one below Monomania. Here you encounter a minor fifth class chimney about 45 feet high. You can boulder it, but consider bringing a short rope to use on the sling fixed there so you can do a body rappel on the way back rather than downclimbing it. Alternately, you can walk around to the left of the chimney over steep, loose rocks that present their own problems.

But is it worth the trip? Probably not unless you are the type that values unique experiences and the thrill of going where few have been. If you're just a casual weekend hiker, enjoy the lower parts of the canyon.

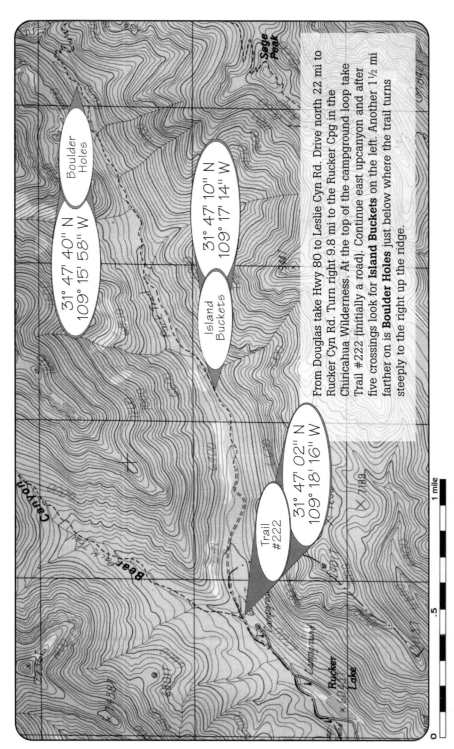

Boulder Holes

31° 47' 40" N
109° 15' 58" W

31° 47' 10" N
109° 17' 14" W

Island Buckets

Trail #222

31° 47' 02" N
109° 18' 16" W

Sage Peak

From Douglas take Hwy 80 to Leslie Cyn Rd. Drive north 22 mi to Rucker Cyn Rd. Turn right 9.8 mi to the Rucker Cpg in the Chiricahua Wilderness. At the top of the campground loop take Trail #222 (initially a road). Continue east upcanyon and after five crossings look for **Island Buckets** on the left. Another 1½ mi farther on is **Boulder Holes** just below where the trail turns steeply to the right up the ridge.

0   .5   1 mile

Rucker Canyon

More tubs than the plumbing section at Home Depot. This part of the creek doesn't have lots of vertical relief, but a pattern of short cascades creates lots of little containers with plenty of surrounding vegetation, and water that's a gorgeous translucent slate color. It's striking in afternoon light.

There are around one dozen closely spaced tubs and pools on the lower section. On this part of the creek the uppermost pool has a collar of rock around the hem that broadens into a sinuous sunning slab. It's more picturesque toward the top, but my picnic blanket goes down on a secluded spot to the left of the trail, across a small island with dappled sunlight. It's not visible from the trail, so privacy is good to excellent.

About one mile farther upstream is another set of cascades. Visually, the best ones are where red rhyolite creates impounds of green water. At another, fractures in the solid rock streambed create a channel that accelerates water and cuts out a hole that's five feet deep and about seven feet in circumference. In addition, there's a picnic area formed by a downed fir that's fallen across the strembed. Floods deposit cobble and sand high up on the stream bank against the trunk and produce a perfectly flat area about the size of a family tent.

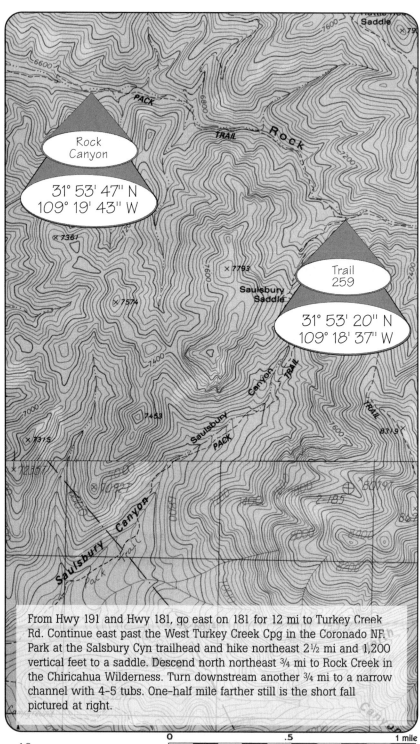

Rock
Canyon

31° 53' 47" N
109° 19' 43" W

Trail
259

31° 53' 20" N
109° 18' 37" W

Saulsbury
Saddle

From Hwy 191 and Hwy 181, go east on 181 for 12 mi to Turkey Creek Rd. Continue east past the West Turkey Creek Cpg in the Coronado NF. Park at the Salsbury Cyn trailhead and hike northeast 2½ mi and 1,200 vertical feet to a saddle. Descend north northeast ¾ mi to Rock Creek in the Chiricahua Wilderness. Turn downstream another ¾ mi to a narrow channel with 4-5 tubs. One-half mile farther still is the short fall pictured at right.

0   .5   1 mile

Rock Canyon

A steep, but not very deep, canyon with a narrowly channeled and fast stream. Lots of loose rock produces cobble and gravel that diminishes depth. It starts getting interesting a little more than one mile after you turn west into Rock Canyon.

The approach is from upstream, and the pools get better the farther downstream you go. A steep rock wall, 80 feet long and covered with moss and lichen, marks a series of dodges and turns in the creek that gouge out a seven-foot pool with two lounging slabs where you can break out the beach towel. Nap in the shade while your fingers drag in the water. In addition, there's a good bench of land ninety vertical feet above the creek that's generally clear of undergrowth and dressed in dappled sunlight. Great place to apply the picnic blanket.

Seventy yards farther down is a larger hole, 20 feet in diameter and oval-shaped. A water chute seven feet high creates a small deep end. There's a good sense of enclosure, not just around the fall itself, but to the south along some rock ledges that are around 15 feet tall with mature Ponderosa and some young oaks.

Expectation of privacy is excellent. Most places have no use trails going down to the stream. Step lightly, this terrain is a great way to injure an ankle.

Why Bother

Tanque Verde Falls
Fewer people at the Arizona versus Arizona State game.

Lower Sabino Canyon
Kid friendly holes right along the paved trail leading north from the visitor's center

Romero Pools
Humdinger of a hole. The upper is fatter and stays good longer into the season. Rope swing and broad slabs to hang out on. Volunteers keep it clean, jumping rocks galore, but 300 visitors on a weekend.

Montrose Pools
Difficult to reach and according to reports, no pool at the bottom.

Cave Creek
Only one bucket. Heavily visited.

Bathtub
Man-made lake. Silted up from fires.

Phoenix Area

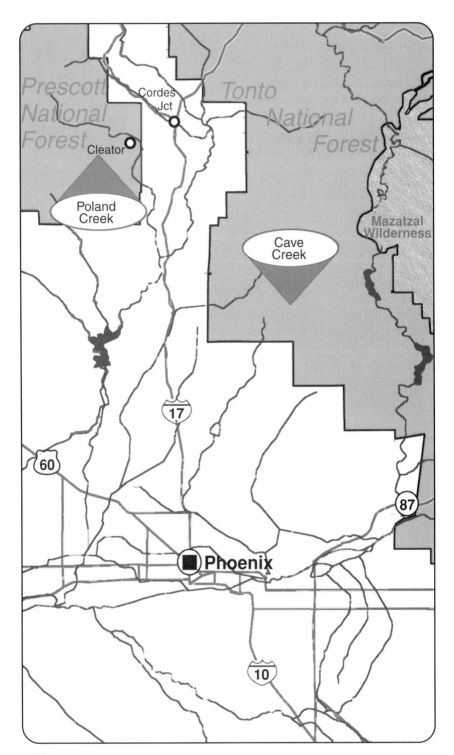

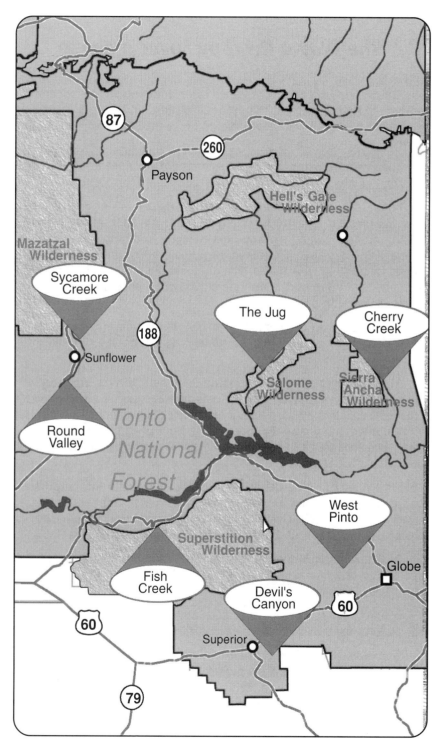

87

260

Payson

Hell's Gate
Wilderness

Mazatzal
Wilderness

Sycamore
Creek

The Jug

Cherry
Creek

188

Sunflower

Salome
Wilderness

Sierra
Ancha
Wilderness

Tonto

Round
Valley

National

Forest

West
Pinto

Superstition
Wilderness

Globe

Fish
Creek

Devil's
Canyon

60

60

Superior

79

51

The Way a Cowboy Loves a Horse

After a winter locals describe as drier than an evangelical convention, spring storms put the sycamores into bud and in a short time fresh young cottonwood leaves would be at their translucent, green climax.

Cherry Creek didn't have many cottonwoods, but I needed to visit anyway. I was looking for a cowboy named Ronnie Manes.

I found Manes last year at the bottom of six miles of bad road. He was wearing a .44 magnum, riding a formerly wild mustang with the U.S. brand and looking like the next casualty in a range war that ended 120 years ago. We talked for at least 40 minutes and the things this little guy with the black hat, shoulder length hair and red bandana said were such authentic cowboy folk wisdom that I remember laughing out loud.

That's about all I remember, though. Notes from the conversation were lost when my truck was burglarized sometime later. I had to find Manes again

At the grocery store in Young, the clerk said he was probably next door at the Valley Bar. She'd call over and ask. I knew I wasn't dressed for a cowboy bar. Patagonia tights clash badly in a room full of Wranglers, but it was too late. While I put my groceries in the truck, Manes was walking across the gravel parking lot to see who was asking for him.

Fifty years of riding horses at high speed over hard ground had put parts of him at odd angles: a broken left wrist, right collar bone, three fractured cervical vertebrae and a wandering left eye earned during an accident with barbed wire when he was 12 years old.

A denture filled the top of his mouth. The bottom plate was apparently at home, while Manes himself had been at the bar for some time.

Inside, I bought him another beer and asked why he wears a felt hat even in the summer.

"First boss I ever had said he wouldn't never hire a cowboy who wore a straw hat or rolled his own cigarettes. He said the cowboy'd either be rolling a smoke or trying to catch his hat when he should be working."

The other men at the bar started to laugh.

"Ronnie," one said, "tell him about the time you tried to cross Cherry Creek when the water was high."

Manes didn't respond so the man decided to tell the story himself.

"He had a 4-wheel drive and he should have made it, but he forgot to lock the hubs. When the truck stalled, he got out and the water carried him a quarter mile before he washed up on a beach. Now somewhere down on Cherry Creek there's a big-mouth bass wearing a set of lower dentures and a black cowboy hat."

Everyone laughed but Manes. After another round I asked if he had any family, but his answer trailed off. So I asked about his horse.

"I don't know that I've had a better horse in my life. You can rope the wildest bull in the morning and that afternoon put a little girl on him and he'll ride her around the ring just as calm as you could imagine."

I asked him the horse's name and he shrugged.

At the moment Manes was riding a backhoe instead of his horse. A dispute with the rancher who previously employed him meant that he was digging holes for septic tanks instead of fence posts. While he was digging a hole one of the new ranch hands came riding up.

"They said they had a bad horse wreck and needed some water. A horse fell down on the ranch's owner. Pinned his leg and they had to cut the horse's throat."

"You ever watch how long an animal thrashes around after you cut its throat? They got three of them there with ropes and they can't get a fallen horse off a man. What kind of cowboy is that? Hell, even if they couldn't get him off, not one of them had a pistol.

It was near closing time and Manes was staring at the empty beer bottle in front of him. His voice was getting high and thin.

"All I know is that when it comes time to kill my horse, somebody else will have to do it." He paused. "Not one of those sons of bitches had a pistol. What kind of cowboy is that?"

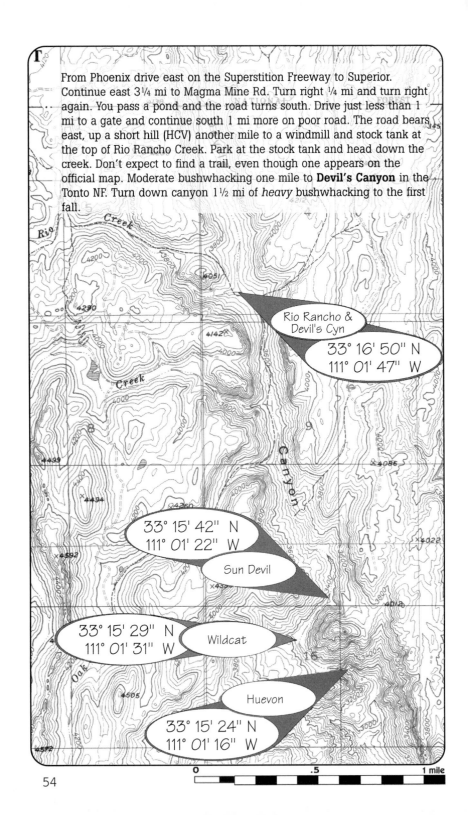

From Phoenix drive east on the Superstition Freeway to Superior.
Continue east 3¼ mi to Magma Mine Rd. Turn right ¼ mi and turn right
again. You pass a pond and the road turns south. Drive just less than 1
mi to a gate and continue south 1 mi more on poor road. The road bears
east, up a short hill (HCV) another mile to a windmill and stock tank at
the top of Rio Rancho Creek. Park at the stock tank and head down the
creek. Don't expect to find a trail, even though one appears on the
official map. Moderate bushwhacking one mile to **Devil's Canyon** in the
Tonto NF. Turn down canyon 1½ mi of *heavy* bushwhacking to the first
fall.

Rio Rancho &
Devil's Cyn

33° 16' 50" N
111° 01' 47" W

33° 15' 42" N
111° 01' 22" W

Sun Devil

33° 15' 29" N
111° 01' 31" W

Wildcat

Huevon

33° 15' 24" N
111° 01' 16" W

0   .5   1 mile

Sun Devil

Here is a series of broad-ass, big-shouldered tanks of water such as mortals seldom see. At the top hole, noonday sun penetrated the smoky emerald water to a depth of 15 feet without hitting the bottom. The tank is 40 feet from wall to wall. Sides are sheer except for a lovely rock terrace. The fall is wide compared to its downstream cousins, but relatively short at a mere 12 feet high. The terrace is on one side of the fall. On the other is a ledge more than 35 feet high.

Five Pools is a rugged approach through about three miles of alder-choked canyons without benefit of a trail. The brush was so thick, I had to wear a helmet. Cat's claw is ubiquitous. Poison oak abounds. You might also need to wade or even swim short portions. In addition to any amphibious gear, sturdy boots and a good hiking pole are strongly recommended. Best if you have bionic knees and a Teflon serape, too. Budget at least three hours of travel time in both directions.

Also, getting to the terrace will require a short, hand-over-hand descent via a rope. There might be one knotted to a tree on the left as you approach from upstream. Better yet, bring 60 feet of line and some runner.

Bonus Feature: Just below the hole is a short slide. It spills into a tub perched right at the lip of the second fall.

Wildcat

Only thing missing is a Slurpee machine. A variety of ledges surround a pool of such perfect oval form that it looks cast by a jeweler. Credit the water with producing the smooth, sinusoidal shape of the waterline. Credit volcanic activity for installing the welded tuff (pronounced toof) 18 million years ago.

It was during a coughing fit in the Miocene Epoch that the Superstition Mountains hacked up a lot of ash which was hardened by the original heat of the volcano into tuff. Typically, extrusive rock is a poor candidate to produce a swimming hole. It's hard, and that's a good thing. But often it's too brittle and when the canyon walls crumble it results in stream beds filled with cobble and boulders. The top of the canyon is like this. But down here the rock seems more resistant and creates vertical walls that rise off the water then bend immediately at 90 degrees to become ledges large enough to host a wedding reception.

Access is by a scrambling trail on the right as you look down canyon. You negotiate the fall via a short down climb on a rope that may or may not be installed. Consider bringing 60 feet of line and a couple of double runners, just in case. For best results wear a good set of sports sandals with sticky rubber on the soles.

Huevos Grandes

Broad as a concert stage, surrounded by a tall curtain of rock, and with a slim fall singing into the center of it. This spot is like a symphony in C major. It's big, big, big. The fall is 50 feet tall. The rock goes up as high as 80 feet, forming an arc of 240 degrees, protecting a tank of water big enough to swim laps in. It's an oval that's got to be 80 feet on the major axis. Depth averages eight feet.

This canyon lends itself more to a one-way, canyoneering style trip than an out and back. Overall it's the toughest place to reach in the whole book. Apart from the flesh-eating plants that line the canyon above, you'll have a sketchy traverse approaching the hole and an even more sketchy rappel to get in. Better eat your Wheaties.

To get there, bypass the upper pools and continue downstream along the rocky rim on the right. Rocks are loose and the potential fall can be 100 feet. Once you get to the ledge overlooking the hole, the only way in is a rappel off the southern wall. Just a little 45-foot slide down the rope. The problem is there's practically nothing to anchor on. Best bet is to bring a standard length rope that you can fix on better rock well back from the drop.

I didn't make the rapp in myself, because I only had a short rope when I visited. This means the anchors recommended above were not tested.

33° 26' 22" N
111° 03' 43" W

West Pinto
Creek

From the town of Superior drive east on Hwy 60 just over 11 mi to a bridge over **West Pinto Creek**. About 1¼ mi farther on, turn north on FS 287, winding through barren tailings from the adjoining mine. Drive 6½ mi to FS 287A in the Tonto NF, turn west just over 4½ mi to some tight switchbacks, and continue another 1¼ mi to clearing beside the creek. Park and continue ¼ mi upstream to hole.

0   .5   1 mile

West Pinto Creek

What gravity gives, it can also take away. This would be a classic swimming hole were it not for a boulder fallen smack in the middle of it. Still, there's plenty of H_2O. It's got vertical walls that rise 25 feet on both sides of water that averages around six feet deep. The surface area of the hole is approximately 20 feet by 30 feet. The sweet spot is eight or nine feet deep and located directly under the left wall where the fall enters the pool. It's awfully narrow here, though. Cliff jumping is risky. Limited seating is also on the left wall, well above the water. Limited shade. This is a well-known swimming hole on the border of the Superstition Wilderness. Basically a drive-up, so be prepared to have neighbors.

If you'd rather have more privacy, consider a tub upstream from the main hole. A five-foot cascade with a submerged collar of rock that creates a modest container. During the season there's a patch of water about four feet deep and just wide enough for a couple if they're hugging one another tightly. Expectation of privacy is guaranteed.

You can take off your clothes once there, but you'll need long sleeves and trousers for the approach. It's a fourth class bushwhack. Shade is sparse and this portion of the creek runs east to west, so lots of sun. This might be a good thing. Since the pool is so small, you'll have to visit early if there's to be flowing water. And it'll be cold. Blazing sun will feel good after a dip.

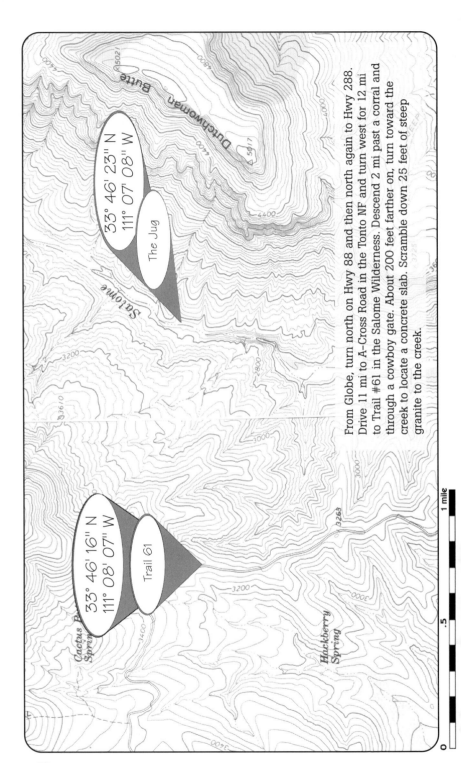

33° 46' 23" N
111° 07' 08" W

The Jug

33° 46' 16" N
111° 08' 07" W

Trail 61

From Globe, turn north on Hwy 88 and then north again to Hwy 288. Drive 11 mi to A-Cross Road in the Tonto NF and turn west for 12 mi to Trail #61 in the Salome Wilderness. Descend 2 mi past a corral and through a cowboy gate. About 200 feet farther on, turn toward the creek to locate a concrete slab. Scramble down 25 feet of steep granite to the creek.

The Jug

Smoothest granite east of the Sierra Nevada. Water pouring out of the Salome Wilderness cuts through an exposed portion of the batholith, a large intrusion of granite that underlies many of the ranges here. It creates a sinuous channel of intriguing shapes. Directly at the bottom of the first access to the creek is a rock that so resembles the torso of a reclining woman that a crack runs directly across her back and shoulders where the bra strap would be. The rest of this miniature canyon has so many sinusoidal curves worn into the rock that you might think yourself in Yosemite except for the saguaro on the canyon walls.

Above, the "sleeping lady" is one of the best late season spots I know of. I say late season because the water is awfully cool in the spring. Also because low levels let you appreciate the beautiful lines of this tub. It's a near-perfect rectangle, twelve feet long, seven feet wide and just as deep. Water exits via a narrow spout etched exquisitely in the rock lip at the bottom of the tub. There is a two-person slab adjoining the pool to the right. An overhanging rock is there if you need some shade.

Warm days in spring can attract as many as one-half dozen cars to the trailhead. Consequently, the canyon can seem busy.

Lower Salome

Canyoneering lite. The gorge here is double diamond steep, but short and with a relatively easy exit. Formed between walls 100 feet high and taller, the creek creates a series of plunge pools that stretch like a string of emeralds for one half mile before terminating in a short, deep narrows. Water creates about one dozen plunge pools carved deep into the granite. Several of them require swimming, but only a couple of strokes. The hole below is another story. It's at the bottom of a 30-foot fall, with sheer granite on either side. The only way in is to rappel down from an anchor on the wall above, or, as most prefer, step off into the air for the two second screamer into the water below.

Directions are simple: put in at the place described on the preceding pages. Then scramble, downclimb and leap for 30 minutes or more to the big drop. Then it's around 100 yards of swimming to the bottom of the narrows. Hike out to the right, scrambling between brush and the rock wall until you intersect the trail that takes you back to the parking.

Like most canyoneering trips, this is done as a one-way excursion. But it's shorter than most, with one optional rappel. No "rescue gully" along the walls, though. As with many canyoneering trips, once you commit, the only way out is through the bottom. Salome Canyon is a good place to test this style of wilderness adventure to decide if you want to tackle longer, more technical trips.

33° 53' 41" N
110° 53' 48" W

Cherry
Falls

Parking

33° 53' 40" N
110° 54' 20" W

Hwy 288 10 mi south of Young, turn east on Road 203. Drive 8¾ mi over washes, loose rock and ruts to a cattle guard. The next wash south of the guard is the descent. Look for a faint, faint trail traveling 400 yds northeast to a gully and a dry fall. Flank to the right, continue bushwhacking downhill 200 ft to a clearing, then veer gently back toward the gully and boulder hop to some rock ledges above **Cherry Creek** in the Sierra Ancha Wilderness. Go downstream on the west side until you wall out about 20 yds above the fall. Cross to the left and you're there. Four-wheel drive highly recommended.

0   .5   1 mile

Cherry Creek

The classic wilderness swimming hole. As remarkable as the surrounding rock faces are, as engaging as the polished ledges, as comforting as the reliable afternoon shade—despite all those charms, the thing that stands out about Cherry Creek Falls is its isolation. It's so far from anything that the best way in is by parachute.

The hole is crescent shaped, around 70 feet from end to end. Most seating is on ledges above the hole. Gobs of smooth rock with an angle that fits any repose. You reach the water by scrambling 15 or so vertical feet and walking out onto a flat, funnel-shaped gravel bar in the middle of the enclosure. Inside the enclosure you can listen to the fall roar during spring runoff or after a good monsoon. If the water level is lower, you can whisper to your companions from 50 feet away and still be heard. Water was cloudy brown when I visited in May and slate green during a later visit in October.

Rock is beautiful, very solid. It creates vertical walls that surround the hole with pale pink collar that is more than 60 feet tall on the left. Most of the rest of the enclosure is 15 to 20 feet high, presenting some ledges with magnificent diving potential. Submerged obstacles seem unlikely, 'cause the bottom appears to be sandy and the good quality of the surrounding rock suggests rock fall is minimal. Better be damned sure you know what you're doing before you jump, 'cause if you frappe, help is a long way off. Get in the water and check it out first.

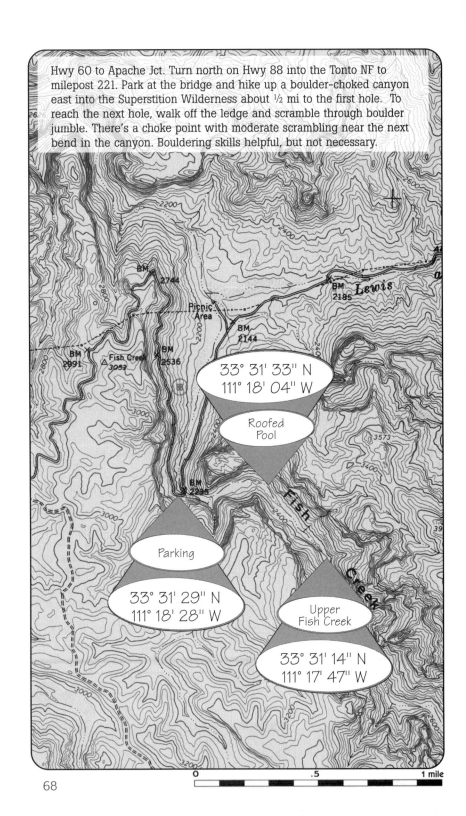

Hwy 60 to Apache Jct. Turn north on Hwy 88 into the Tonto NF to milepost 221. Park at the bridge and hike up a boulder-choked canyon east into the Superstition Wilderness about ½ mi to the first hole. To reach the next hole, walk off the ledge and scramble through boulder jumble. There's a choke point with moderate scrambling near the next bend in the canyon. Bouldering skills helpful, but not necessary.

33° 31' 33" N
111° 18' 04" W

Roofed
Pool

Parking

33° 31' 29" N
111° 18' 28" W

Upper
Fish Creek

33° 31' 14" N
111° 17' 47" W

0   .5   1 mile

Fish Creek

A lush canyon for all levels of hiker. The first spot has a glorious camping bench. There's a tub nearby that's remarkable in that a massive boulder overhangs it so far that it's almost roofed. Tremendous views downstream of tall, red rock walls, cottonwood and Arizona walnut. In sum, a place to take it in, but not to jump in because it appears this tub gets sluggish early.

Upstream is a beautiful pool, 20 feet in diameter and deeper than I could tell. That's because there is no easy way out once you're in unless you bring a rope, and I didn't have one with me. There's also a rock shaped like a high-back love seat. It offers some extra lounging privacy since it faces upstream, thus shielding the inhabitants from visitors approaching from downstream, or at least allowing some warning before they arrive.

There's another hole up above the bend in the canyon. It's a place of perpetual shade with a good collection of cottonwoods and big, high walls all around. The pool here is about 35 feet long, and maybe 6 feet deep at the top. The flow is lower because the stream is split by a large boulder. Best place to park it is under a big ol' cottonwood lodged across the water.

Beautiful emerald water early in the year, but it can get sluggish between spring runoff and the monsoon. It's a popular trail, so be prepared to make room for others, particularly at the lower spots.

33° 51' 16" N
111° 27' 17" W

Parking

33° 50' 51" N
111° 27' 38" W

Second Pool

First Pool

33° 50' 50" N
111° 27' 25" W

From Pheonix take Hwy 87 north to Sunflower, turn right at "Bushnell Tanks" on FS 22 in the Mazatzal Mtns. Drive to the third crossing, park and head down the creek to a gauging station. Shortly below you encounter the main hole. Continue .3 mi downstream to where the creek bends east for the second hole. The third hole is another ¼ mi.

0   .5   1 mile

Sycamore Creek

Forget a flotation vest, bring a bulletproof one. To reach this pool you have to walk through a heavily visited swimming hole where I counted four different types of shell casings. But if you don't mind a little bushwhacking and some ricochets you can find a place down-stream with better privacy.

The first one is just below the main hole. It's a slot more than 8 feet long that's fat at the center and maybe as deep as 12 feet. Additionally, there's a gently sloping sand beach that's to die for. The beach is guarded by a dozen willow trees and backed by a rock wall 25 feet high. One of the prettiest beaches anywhere. I didn't know whether to stand and applaud or sit down and cry. Get there early and stake out primo location on the beach.

The next pool is about one-quarter mile farther down canyon. It's just above a small arroyo entering from the north. It's formed in a small constriction with a sand and cobble bottom. Lots of boulders scattered around, too. Not a diving spot, but deep enough that the average NBA player could go in up to his armpits. The beach is cobbles and boulders, too. No comfortable place to lie down, but there's still a really cool place to perch. It's on a tree where one of the trunks makes a nice elbow a couple of feet off the ground, perfect to climb up in and kick back for some reading. There are a couple of oaks for shade and even some saguaros downstream.

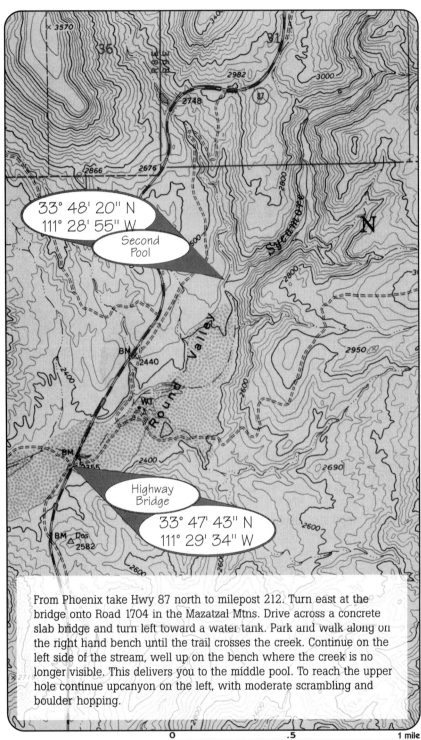

33° 48' 20" N
111° 28' 55" W

Second Pool

Highway Bridge

33° 47' 43" N
111° 29' 34" W

From Phoenix take Hwy 87 north to milepost 212. Turn east at the bridge onto Road 1704 in the Mazatzal Mtns. Drive across a concrete slab bridge and turn left toward a water tank. Park and walk along on the right hand bench until the trail crosses the creek. Continue on the left side of the stream, well up on the bench where the creek is no longer visible. This delivers you to the middle pool. To reach the upper hole continue upcanyon on the left, with moderate scrambling and boulder hopping.

0   .5   1 mile

Round Valley

There are three swimming spots on this part of the creek where the tight walls relax enough to allow pools that are good to excellent. The best one is at the top, farthest from the trailhead. It's around 60 feet long, bounded on the left by a 10-foot wall, with the beach at bottom right. Depth is limited due to boulder clutter. A second, more accessible basin is located a few hundred feet below. Once again, depth is limited.

In Round Valley I thought that I found a great hiding place. But within a couple of minutes some bathers showed up who were hiding nothing. This is a major nudist spot. If you arrive during nude recreation week in July, you might find as many as 20 folks at this otherwise little-visited pool along the old stage route between Payson and Phoenix.

It also has the best beaches in the state, gorgeous little sand pockets nourished by seasonal floods and preserved by loosely clustered shade trees. Among these is an intimate spot farther downstream from the rest. Here, a narrow pool about 60 feet long forms against a wall. Depth is limited by the sandy bottom, but the spot is totally enclosed and is reached not by the trail, but by bush-whacking and boulder hopping a short distance upstream from the bridge. Privacy here is excellent to guaranteed.

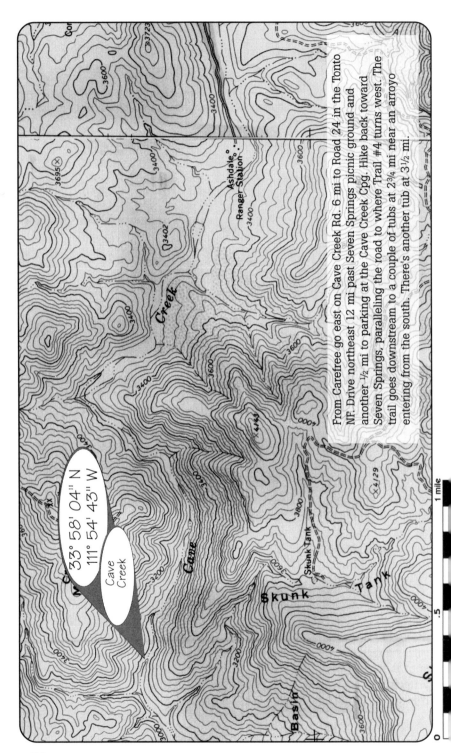

From Carefree go east on Cave Creek Rd. 6 mi to Road 24 in the Tonto NF. Drive northeast 12 mi past Seven Springs picnic ground and another ½ mi to parking at the Cave Creek Cpg. Hike back toward Seven Springs, paralleling the road to where Trail #4 turns west. The trail goes downstream to a couple of tubs at 2¾ mi near an arroyo entering from the south. There's another tub at 3½ mi.

33° 58' 04" N
111° 54' 43" W

Cave Creek

Skunk Tank

Skunk Tank

Ashdale Ranger Station

Basin

Cave Creek

The sweetest place to sit in the whole state of Arizona. There's a perfectly flat stone the size of a park bench right next to a tiny waterfall. A juniper provides a low, dense canopy of shade that'll keep you cool when the surrounding vegetation is at the flash point. The adjoining pool occurs where a handful of large boulders have tumbled across the stream. As it rushes over the boulders, the water accelerates just enough to scrape a modest pool out of the sand and gravel streambed. The pool is circular, about 30 feet in diameter, but none too deep, maybe six feet in the center although this will vary with water level and the amount of cobble in the creek bed.

Lots of people with side arms, it seemed. Rationally I know that the reason people carry combat automatics into the mountains is because they are more afraid of you than you should be of them...this or they believe that rattlesnakes attack in packs. Still, I got a kind of weird vibe and I'm a gun owner myself.

Aside from the firearm notice, be advised to bring something to sit on because the rocks are dark and will get very hot during mid-day. Also, it's a short steep descent with loose rock. A walking stick is recommended.

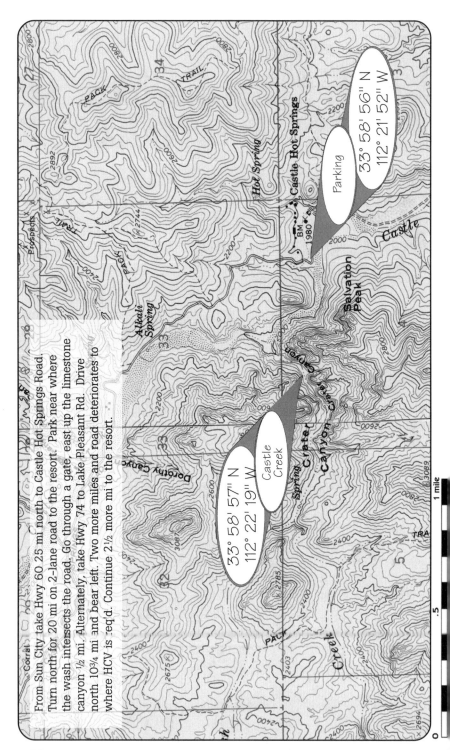

From Sun City take Hwy 60 25 mi north to Castle Hot Springs Road. Turn north for 20 mi on 2-lane road to the resort. Park near where the wash intersects the road. Go through a gate, east up the limestone canyon ½ mi. Alternately, take Hwy 74 to Lake Pleasant Rd. Drive north 10¾ mi and bear left. Two more miles and road deteriorates to where HCV is req'd. Continue 2½ more mi to the resort.

Parking

33° 58' 56" N
112° 21' 52" W

Castle Creek

33° 58' 57" N
112° 22' 19" W

Castle Creek

A tall eastern wall decorated with penstemons produces a serpentine slot about 6 feet wide and filled to a depth of about 7 feet with crystal clear water. At the top is a short fall mediated by a boulder that fits into a slot like a key in the hole. There's a great sense of enclosure here, so much so that voices echo. The slot is north facing, shady and cool. A pretty little sand beach 150-200 square feet on the right of the keyhole presents about the only place to stretch out. Rock surrounding the slot is about 15 feet high. It might be jumpable depending on water levels. The sandy bottom means that if you hit, you wouldn't break your leg too badly.

Another slot pool farther up has even nicer contours, but steeper sides make it less user friendly. You'll find no practical way out unless you fasten 30 feet of rope onto a cable left by miners and hand over hand back out.

To get to these places you have to cross a spur of private property owned by the Castle Creek Hotsprings. Caretaker Mike Doughtery said it's permitted, but policy can change. Doughtery also said that John Kennedy spent some time at the springs recovering from his war wounds.

"Every once in awhile we catch a whiff of something sweet smelling," Doughtery said. "Like perfume. We don't have any flowers around here, so we figure it must be JFK chasing Marilyn Monroe's ghost around."

From Phoenix take I-17 north to Bloody Basin. Exit on Road 259 and drive 18 mi toward Crown King into the Bradshaw Mountains and the Castle Creek Wilderness. About 2 mi before Crown King, look for a turn out on right and Trail #225, the Algonquin Trail. Descend 1¼ mi and about 1,000 vertical feet to the creek. Turn downstream ¼ mi. to the confluence of Hell's Hole Cyn, and 400 feet farther on is the hole of the same name. **Cottonwood Tank** and **Big Dipper** are 1,000 feet downstream from this.

34° 13' 03" N
112° 18' 25" W

Algonquin Trail

34° 12' 52" N
112° 17' 47" W

Big Dipper

Poland Creek

34° 12' 47" N
112° 18' 12" W

0   .5   1 mile

Hell's Hole

Poland Creek has about six places worth taking your shorts off. At the bottom of the trail are some shallow pools created by falls less than 6 feet high. They're only fair. A little more than one-quarter mile farther on is a good pool. A couple of hundred yards downstream from that is another good pool, right at the confluence of a tributary that enters from the right. And, a little more than one-half mile up the tributary is a series of pools that are good to excellent. All of these are intriguing at first, but not in the same league with the three holes downstream that are reviewed on the following pages.

The first eye popper is about 100 yards downstream from the confluence mentioned above. It's 35 feet long, 12 feet wide and easily seven feet deep. The shape is generally rectangular and there are some potential jumps from small ledges, but the vertical is no more than 8 feet. The hole is fed by a cascade that's just average on the aesthetic scale. A tall smooth boulder at the top of the cascade is perfect seating for two and it's right under a small tree that gives good afternoon shade.

Getting in and out of the water is problematic, though. The sides of the container aren't very tall, but they're steep and slick.

Big Dipper

Big Dipper

Big Dipper is a hole of epic proportions. A 35-foot fall spills into a container of near vertical rock. The head is a steep, deeply polished slab where water pours over in a broad sheet, filling a pool that is 60 to 70 feet across. Big walls slide down into water that's at least 10 feet deep, probably more, depending on water levels in the Bradshaw Mountains.

All of the jumps have ledges that are difficult to reach and at an angle that requires jumpers to get plenty of clearance in order to hit water instead of rock. Scrambling back to the top is impossible without a rope fixed beforehand. The hem of the pool has some shade from slender trees over an uneven chunk of rock directly across from the fall. Other than that, parking is limited.

Big Dipper is no more than a couple of hundred yards below Hell's Hole. Once you get to the lip of the fall, bear left over a rocky shoulder out of view of the creek. Getting down to the pool requires some fourth class scrambling on loose rock and a couple of fifth class moves. If you have any climbing experience you can make it without belay and even an average athletic person can do the downclimb without incident, but the prudent thing is to use a body belay.

Sycamore Creek

Cottonwood Tank

So nice, you'll want to settle down and have your mail forwarded here. While not nearly as well bounded as Hell's Hole it's a little fatter and more round, plus the low walls make it more user friendly. What's more, a mature cottonwood at the top gives this hole the best shade on Poland Creek. Like Hell's Hole, this pool faces northeast. Water splits at the top and enters through twin chutes. During moderate levels, the water runs across a gently sloped piece of rock and creates a lounging slab next to the running water and within the deep shade of the cottonwood. Just beautiful.

You'll be able to enjoy yourself with more confidence if you take the precaution of not leaving valuables in your vehicle. I know this because my truck was burglarized here. The trailhead for Poland Creek is right on the road to Crown King. Thieves know that when you park at the top of the trail, you'll be gone for some time. They can see down the trail, in the event that hikers are returning, plus they can see or hear approaching cars easily.

In the end this trip to Poland Creek cost me a couple thousand dollars in lost gear. But subtract that from the value of discovering this marvelous canyon and my balance sheet is still in the black.

Why Bother

Six Shooter Canyon
More buckets than a janitor's closet. The lower stream is characterized by short falls that empty into boulder filled buckets. From Globe follow signs toward the forest service station. Before the station turn right on Sixshooter Canyon Road to Trail 197.

Lower Salt River Cyn
Forest Service 303 to the river, then upstream just over one mile to Ash Creek. Major party spot.

The Pool/Queen Creek
Really cool sport climbing routes directly above the fall, but also right by SR 60. Not a hiking destination.

The Mogollon Rim

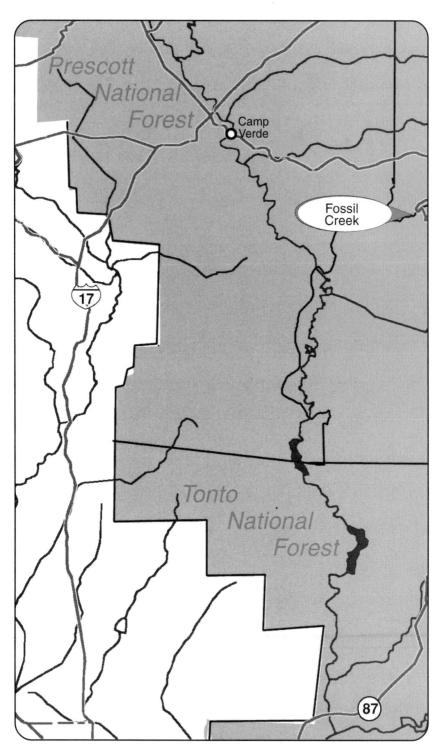

Prescott
National
Forest

Camp
Verde

Fossil
Creek

17

Tonto
National
Forest

87

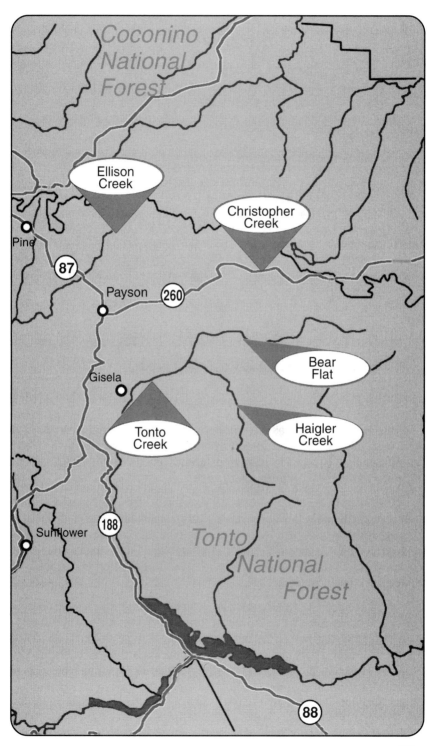

Coconino National Forest

Ellison Creek

Christopher Creek

Pine

87

Payson 260

Bear Flat

Gisela

Tonto Creek

Haigler Creek

Sunflower 188

Tonto National Forest

88

Buzz Worms

It was raining hard, so I stopped at a restaurant. This was not in the desert, but a couple of years earlier when I was in the Pacific Northwest. The restaurant was virtually empty, so after the woman minding the counter took my order, we talked about hiking and swimming holes.

"Isn't it dangerous out there? You never worry about bears?"

The waitress from Wenatchee was expressing the regional version of a universal fear. Whether it's bears in the Northwest, mountain lions in California, alligators in Florida or deputy sheriffs in rural Georgia, everybody has a primal fear that some predator will make them the hapless loser in the ancient drama of man versus nature.

In the Southwest, that animal is the rattlesnake. Oh, sure. You've got your Gila Monsters. I was talking to some old men in a cafe. One was telling a story about Gila monsters.

"Do you run across the lizards very often?" I asked the Old Fart.

"Yep," he said. "Every time I see one, I run across it."

Road kill is part of the reason that the beaded lizards are rare and leave the role of local menace to the rattlesnake.

There are as many as one dozen species and sub species of rattler native to the Southwest. Mojave Greens, Sidewinders, Western Diamondbacks. To look at the color photos in the field guides, you'd think there's a snake under every rock.

The truth is that you can spend months in the Southwest without seeing a rattlesnake. They're shy, with the possible exception of a couple of weeks in spring when they're coming out of torpor and looking hard for a meal. Even so, a person is 50,000 times more likely to shake hands with the President than be bitten by a rattle-snake.

Neither species of belly crawler was on my mind one afternoon while speeding down a narrow trail on a mountain bike. On the left was a jagged rock wall. On the right, a steep slope falling 200 feet to the river below. I accelerated out of the curve and there, stretched between the two hazards, was the Pappa Daddy pit viper two seconds from my front wheel. At that proximity he looked as thick as a irrigation pipe.

Three options: Flesh wounds to the left, fractures to the right or a neurotoxin down the middle. If I crashed, my feet might stay clipped to the pedals, leaving me hog tied and at eye level with a serpent big enough to have his own ZIP code. Ride over him and he was apt to flex spasmodically and wrap around my ankle or my bike.

"Do snakes become angry when they're tangled in wheel spokes," I wondered?

Yes, I decided.

In the clarity sometimes inspired by panic, I devised a fourth option and with stiff shoulders and trembling legs, I lifted both wheels in the air, hopped over the snake and landed without looking back.

That week I encountered more rattlesnakes than during the combined 10 months it took to research this book. And the best story didn't even involve a snake.

I was crouching and thrashing through heavy brush at the edge of a stream when a branch lodged between my pack and torso, then broke off there. There was a yard-long willow limb sticking out behind me, but I was too busy looking for creatures with rattles to notice my own tail, until I got to a clearing and stood up straight.

The branch hit the back of my legs and my response was limbic. I bolted, high-stepping and hyper-ventilating for 50 feet. Each step forward I could feel the scaly creature reaching for my trailing leg. This cartoon continued until the branch dislodged and I was able to resume thinking with my cortex.

The cortex is the part of the brain I used earlier to tell the waitress from Wenatchee that no, I was not afraid of bears.

"The most dangerous thing I do is drive to the trailhead," I told her.

But fear usually isn't rational and imagination inclines toward the dramatic. The likelihood of being sent to the everafter by a family sedan just doesn't excite the senses the way a predator does. It also explains why you'll never see a terrified man running down a trail and swatting himself in the ass with a Buick.

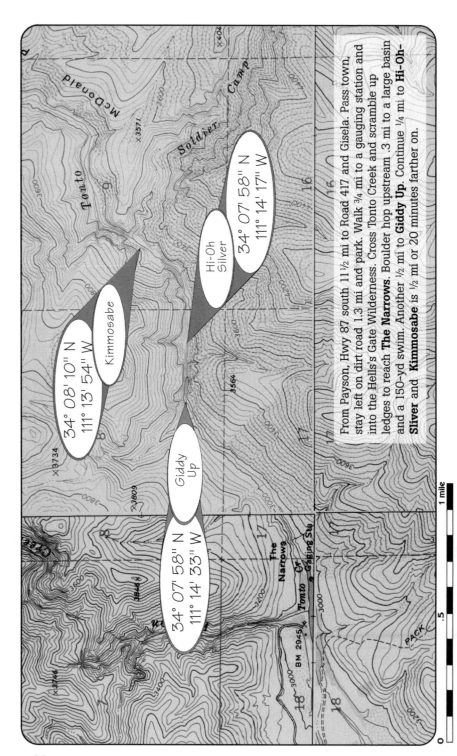

34° 08' 10" N
111° 13' 54" W

Kimmosabe

Hi-Oh Silver

34° 07' 58" N
111° 14' 17" W

Giddy Up

34° 07' 58" N
111° 14' 33" W

The Narrows

Gaging Site

BM 2945

From Payson, Hwy 87 south 11½ mi to Road 417 and Gisela. Pass town, stay left on dirt road 1.3 mi and park. Walk ¾ mi to a gauging station and into the Hells's Gate Wilderness. Cross Tonto Creek and scramble up ledges to reach **The Narrows**. Boulder hop upstream .3 mi to a large basin and a 150-yd swim. Another ½ mi to **Giddy Up**. Continue ¼ mi to **Hi-Oh-Sliver** and **Kimmosabe** is ½ mi or 20 minutes farther on.

1 mile

.5

0

Giddy Up

More pigeons than people. Big walls create nesting spots like in an urban high-rise. This part of the canyon is much more like a narrows than the overrun swimming hole downstream known as the "The Narrows." The left wall is 100 feet high and sheer. Rock on the right is not nearly as high, but presents its own challenge, more of which later. The pool is 50 feet long and 20 feet wide with a little fall at the top.

Depth is overhead in most places, but scattered boulders make that factor variable. That same boulder clutter is also responsible for the fall at the top of the slot. The only jumping ledge is adjacent to the fall. This is also the spot where you climb 15 feet up and around to reach the holes reviewed in the following pages.

To get around the fall you have to climb one of the cracks on the right. The one that appears to be the easiest isn't. Instead, move a few feet farther upstream and start on a crack about 15 feet down-stream from the fall. The climb is not more than a couple of moves. The difficulty is around 5.4. But remember, you'll be doing this with wet hands and feet. For non-climbers in the group, somebody who does have rock gear should bring a #7 or #8 stopper for something to grab on.

Note: Usability is a problem. There's no comfortable place to sit other than on cobbles at the lower end and the only shade comes from your hat brim.

Hi-Oh-Silver

The main feature is not the swimming hole itself (which is really nice) but a smooch seat and snuggle shelf carved out of the granite wall on the left side. The seat is more like an out-sized reclining chair with upswept sides and a tall back that provides privacy in the unlikely event of visitors approaching from downstream. It's just a killer spot to be with your love interest.

The snuggle shelf is about the size of a large dinner table. During low water it will be raised a little more than a foot above the water line. It's smooth and the horizontal surface is slightly concave and filled with sand and small gravel. If you're rugged, a towel should be all you need to lie on. However, if you anticipate more pressure might be applied consider bringing a sleeping pad to keep the rocks from poking you or yours in the back.

The hole itself is a pretty oval shape about 60 feet long. The bottom is clear with no boulder clutter and a fat deep end. The left wall is around 80 feet tall. Best thing about Tonto Creek here is that it's a low water spot. Visit during dry years or on either side of the monsoon season, late spring or early autumn. Big, big afternoon sun with only the barest shade at the bottom of the pool under some immature willows and a sycamore.

Kimmosabe

More vertical walls, more long water. The hole is a damn sight longer than an Olympic pool. Depth will average about six feet, but that can change season to season since it's a spot that appears to collect lots of sand. Regardless, it's a great place to blow bubbles. I swam laps for the better part of an hour and my only complaint was there was no stripe painted on the bottom.

Midway through, the bottom rises to become little more than waist deep and paradoxically that's where the fun begins. On the left is a small gravel bar, 15 feet long and hard up against the left wall. A fringe of alders turns it into a bed with a curtain of privacy drawn around it. It's especially precious since it's so rare to find a beach– much less trees –smack in the center of a sheer rock where the flow runs hard during high water. There is even more shade at the bottom of the hole under sycamore and alders.

One caution—it's best to approach from the left bank rather than directly upstream through the mud and vegetation at the bottom of the hole. This because riparian habitat is sensitive and lots of little critters need it to survive in a climate that doesn't favor water loving species. Tread carefully.

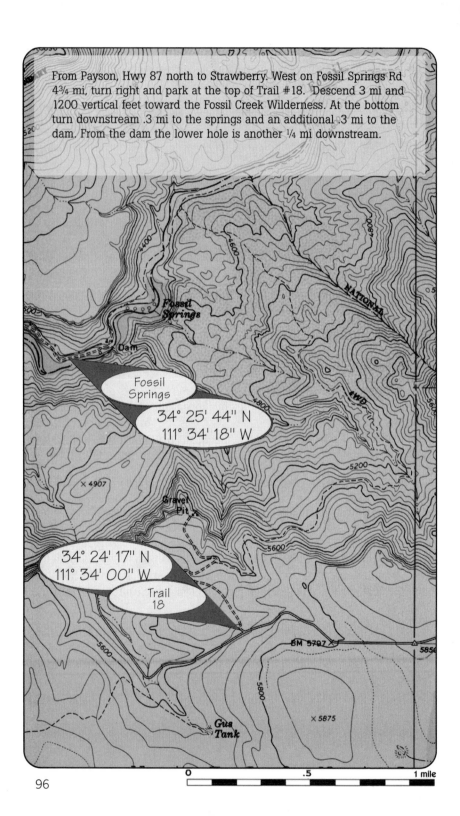

From Payson, Hwy 87 north to Strawberry. West on Fossil Springs Rd 4¾ mi, turn right and park at the top of Trail #18. Descend 3 mi and 1200 vertical feet toward the Fossil Creek Wilderness. At the bottom turn downstream .3 mi to the springs and an additional .3 mi to the dam. From the dam the lower hole is another ¼ mi downstream.

Fossil Springs

Dam

Fossil
Springs
34° 25' 44" N
111° 34' 18" W

× 4907

Gravel
Pit

34° 24' 17" N
111° 34' 00" W

Trail
18

BM 5797

Gas
Tank

× 5875

0   .5   1 mile

Fossil Dam

At the dam below the main spring there's a super deep pool. The most interesting feature is in the rock to the right of the main current. The creek apparently bored a wide hole so deep that it forms a short underwater passage connecting to the main channel of the creek. The passage is around five feet under water and about six-feet long.

There are some spots where you can find privacy on Fossil Creek. This isn't one of them. On a holiday weekend you can expect to find as many as 50 cars parked at the trailhead. David Stover of Mesa tells what he witnessed one Labor Day.

"There was a brand new, black BMW. A big one. This woman got out of the car and put on a new pair of hiking boots, I mean the kind of boots you could do Everest in. Meanwhile the guy stayed in the car, air-conditioning on, motor running. When she finished, they walked about 100 feet down the trail and had lunch. That was their Labor Day weekend hike."

Most visitors *do* make it to the springs, however. It takes one hour to descend about four miles and 1,700 feet from the trail above. If you approach from the bottom along the Flume Road it's a little shorter and only about 1,000 vertical feet of hiking.

Fossil Springs

Impossibly lush. A spring produces more than 15,000 gallons of mineral rich water each minute. These deep holes of clear, blue water at a constant temperature of 72 degrees are among the best loved swimming holes in the Southwest and generations of visitors are evident in the soil erosion around tree roots.

And it's not just people. Many visitors bring their dogs. Officially it's discouraged and in most cases it is a bad idea for the dogs. The rocky trail is like torture for pads accustomed to nothing rougher than park grass. However, some exceptions should be made: Take Oscar, a pit bull mix.

"He was a pound dog. My mom got him as a Christmas gift for me," said Steven Aaird of Phoenix. "He started jumping off the rocks with us. He's like that. He sees us doing something and he wants to try it." Then Oscar saw them use the rope swing. "Every time we come here he gets better and better," Aaird said.

Oscar lunges from the bank, seizes the rope in his jaws and swings out into the water. At his best, he can create a six-foot arc before releasing. Other times he hangs on for the ride, paddling swiftly at the air for a minute or more. Then he'll drop and do it again and again and again

"Last time I had to make him stop. His gums were getting all bloody."

Lower Fossil

A swimming hole that smiles back at you. It's an oval approximately 50 feet long with a gravel bottom that rises smoothly to the end of the pool. What makes it so delightful, apart from the lovely color of the water on Fossil Creek, is the contour of the hole. The top of the pool is bordered by a large boulder on the left that's approximately 15 feet high. The rest of the arc is completed by a set of ledges that look as if they were drawn with a compass. The upper tier rises above the water at an average height of 20 inches. The lower tier is submerged, creating a crescent that looks like a travertine grin.

The water is deep enough for shallow dives from the ledges at the top. The boulder on the left is difficult to climb and the water isn't deep enough for jumps anyway. The hole isn't visible from the nearby road, so it escapes most traffic. Expectation of privacy is excellent.

Ledges, logs and undercuts on this part of the stream are important habitat for many species. A couple of soft-shell turtles live here, among other critters. In addition to the usual admonitions about not tramping grass, here's one bit of etiquette you might not have considered. Wildlife biologist Cheryl Carrothers at the Payson Ranger District advises that you not turn over rocks. Reptiles, insects, spiders and small mammals rely upon this type of cover, she said. And that's part of a turtle's diet.

Turn
Right
34° 21' 31" N
111° 16' 50" W

Swimming
Hole
34° 21' 07" N
111° 16' 40" W

From Payson take Hwy 87 northwest 2 mi to Houston Mesa Rd (#199) and go 8 mi north to the second crossing of the East Verde River in the Tonto NF. Turn right ¼ mi after the crossing and park. Walk along road past locked gate approximately .3 mi to a short spur trail that leads to Ellison Creek. Walk up slabs 200 yds to the fall.

0 .5 1 mile

Ellison Creek

A weekday classic, also referred to as Cold Springs. Broad granite slabs play home to one-half dozen pools. The premier spot is at the bottom of a two-tier fall that's about 40 feet high. The tank is 35 feet across and around eight feet deep in the center. My favorite feature is a dynamite sunning rock at the bottom of hole. A huge tree trunk is wedged parallel to the fall and has some steps cut into it. No real purpose to the steps, you can't dive from it since the water's not nearly deep enough. It's just something to scramble around on, fall and get injured.

The trunk probably washed down after a 1990 fire that burned 24,000 acres at the top of the watershed. Dead trees and disturbed soil tumbled downstream, depositing lots of silt in this otherwise deep hole. Officials reseeded the burn area immediately, but say it still took two years before the siltation even slowed down. Since then they planted trees, but it will be many years before restoration is complete and places like Ellison Creek reach normal depth.

Pity the person who arrives here on "senior ditch day." Ellison Creek is a high school party spot. Many fire rings and broken bottles at the parking site. There are also some steep pools on the East Verde just below the road crossing. Pretty, but who wants to swim in water that minutes before was rinsing hubcaps on cattle trucks?

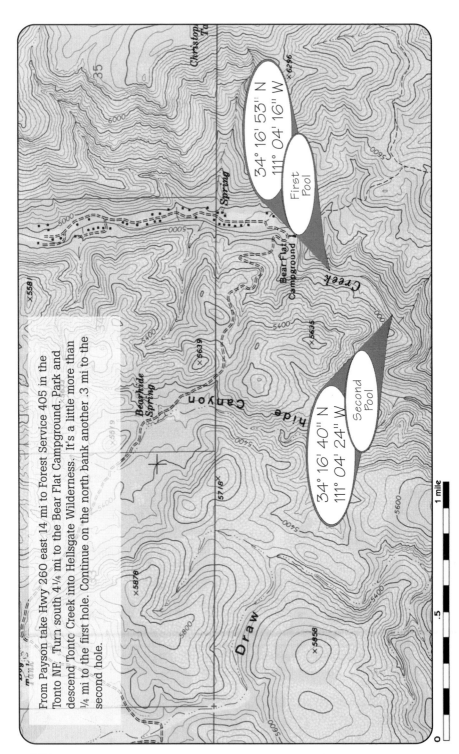

From Payson take Hwy 260 east 14 mi to Forest Service 405 in the Tonto NF. Turn south 4¼ mi to the Bear Flat Campground. Park and descend Tonto Creek into Hellsgate Wilderness. It's a little more than ¼ mi to the first hole. Continue on the north bank another .3 mi to the second hole.

First Pool

34° 16' 53" N
111° 04' 16" W

Second Pool

34° 16' 40" N
111° 04' 24" W

Bear Flat

The pinkest granite in the Southwest. Centuries of spring runoff from the Mogollon Rim has shaped rock into smooth, pre-Cambrian lounge chairs. There are two spots to visit here. At the top is an enchanting pool with emerald water collected underneath a mammoth ledge large enough for a circus tent. Downstream are the aforementioned lounge chairs. Water pools most notably in a tank that's 45 feet long and 15 feet wide. The seats face upstream, so you will be pointed into the current as you sip your afternoon cocktail and consider what to have for supper.

Local resident Ron Tofoya recommends crawfish. Tonto Creek is thick with them—a delicacy—and that's not just his opinion. On one trip to the creek Tofoya set a group of scouts to work collecting the crustaceans.

"There was probably six or seven pounds. I cooked them with some red wine, onions and chili. I guess everybody liked them 'cause there wasn't nothing leftover."

Catching the critters by hand might be a good way to keep a group of pre-adolescents busy. An option is to trap them using a section of hardware cloth and a piece of bacon securely fastened to the center of it. Attach string to each corner of the cloth so that you can lift the screen out of the water after a suitable number of crayfish have crawled to the bait.

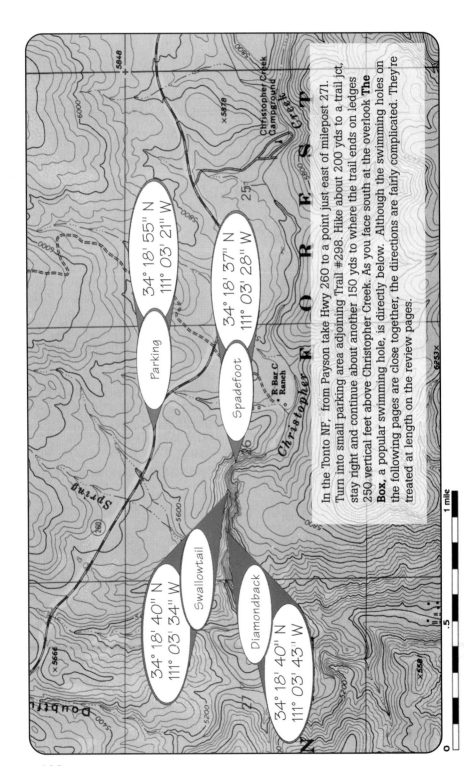

In the Tonto NF, from Payson take Hwy 260 to a point just east of milepost 271. Turn into small parking area adjoining Trail #298. Hike about 200 yds to a trail jct, stay right and continue about another 150 yds to where the trail ends on ledges 250 vertical feet above Christopher Creek. As you face south at the overlook **The Box,** a popular swimming hole, is directly below. Although the swimming holes on the following pages are close together, the directions are fairly complicated. They're treated at length on the review pages.

Parking

34° 18' 55" N
111° 03' 21" W

Spadefoot

34° 18' 37" N
111° 03' 28" W

Swallowtail

34° 18' 40" N
111° 03' 34" W

Diamondback

34° 18' 40" N
111° 03' 43" W

Christopher Creek Campground

CHRISTOPHER FOREST

Spring

R-Bar C Ranch

0   .5   1 mile

Spadefoot

A couple of holes located at the bottom of a steep, rocky descent. Lots of traversing ledges and downstepping. At the canyon bottom the rock bed is angled at 15 degrees toward the stream flow. The result is smooth, expansive slabs that create perhaps the best spot to sun in this book. Entry and exit are simple. Shade is sparse. The best tactic for a summer day is dunk, dry, repeat.

From the overlook, take a moment to examine the 300-foot tall canyon wall. Ledges begin downstream, then slope toward you. To reach "B" and the holes reviewed on following pages, you need to bushwhack downstream along the terraces.

Because of the way those terraces are angled, you must bush-whack and scramble to a point above and downstream from the destination. Then walk the ledge in the upstream direction, descending toward the destination. Although this is rugged, rugged country, the paths are easier to follow than I imagined. That's not to say clear.

Vertical scrambles of 15 feet may be necessary and you may need to rely on route-finding skills. Close examination will show disturbed soil and minor evidence of trodden grass. Where travel up and down rock chutes is indicated, you'll notice small areas of rock polished to a light brown by contact of hands and feet.

Box Canyon

Swallowtail

This waypoint marks a pair of holes. The first (not pictured) is a plunge pool. The fall is a single chute, around 15 feet high and angled to the left as you look up canyon. Water exits over one layer of rock, falls seven feet, bounces off a ledge and falls another seven feet into a pool. The water at the bottom is around 40 feet long and bounded on the downstream end by a spit of cobble and gravel substantial enough to support a modest growth of low trees. Not the best place to sit, though. Better to stretch out on rock slabs next to the fall, and you can walk right down into the water. No dives, though. The right wall is too steep and narrow to clamber up onto.

The lower pool is 120 feet below the first. It's comprised of three pools, none of them good enough to merit a review. But the cascade at the top along with a couple of potential slides that connect the pools are really pretty.

First the cascade. It's up at the top of the series. Water enters through a chute maybe two feet wide, then splits into a hundred pieces. The rock below is a wedding cake five tiers tall that creates a horsetail fall 15 feet wide at the bottom. Of the slides, the middle one has the best potential and the pool it empties into is about three times larger than its upstream cousins.

Diamondback

This marks four holes, closely spaced with each one bigger than the next. At the top is a hole with a cabin-sized boulder on the left and a nice sycamore tree next to the boulder. A rope is fixed on the wall just behind the boulder, suggesting it was placed for mounting the rock and jumping.

The middle is a twin fall that has the rarest of things, shade. Willows cover the cobble beach directly across from the fall. Shade is also available to the left under a ledge that shelters a smooth slab. Very nice. The pool is about 50 feet wide and 30 feet long. The depth probably won't be that great since the impound is created by a cobble beach. That said, there are some really tempting jumping rocks about 15 feet high directly between the falls.

The third feature is a plunge pool with sheer walls that top out on a terrace about 50 feet above the water. The fall that feeds it is the same height. Depth in the pool is undetermined, but you can bet it's profound. Reach it via a minor, 90-foot chimney. You can probably downclimb it, but I used a rope, 'cause I'm a sissy.

The lower fall (shown opposite) is the biggest pool so far. Walls rise from the bottom of the fall for 130 feet. A tall, proud fall lands in a funnel-shaped pool, about 70 feet long. Getting there is difficult. I photographed from above, although it appears there's an approach leading down to it from where I stood.

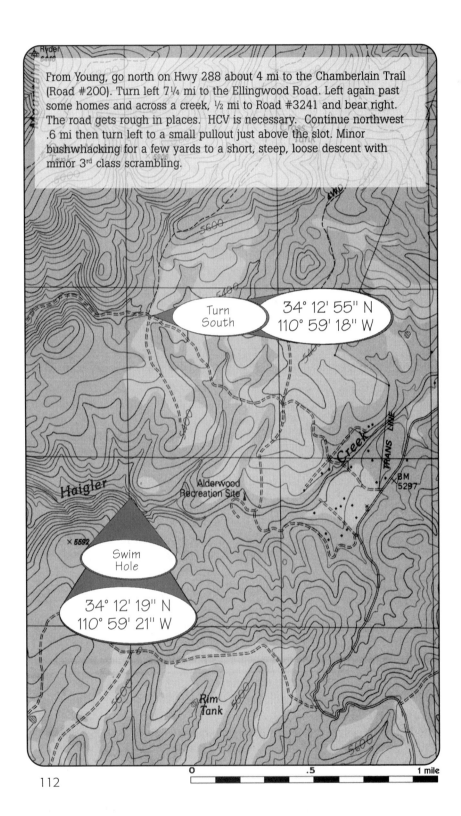

From Young, go north on Hwy 288 about 4 mi to the Chamberlain Trail (Road #200). Turn left 7¼ mi to the Ellingwood Road. Left again past some homes and across a creek, ½ mi to Road #3241 and bear right. The road gets rough in places. HCV is necessary. Continue northwest .6 mi then turn left to a small pullout just above the slot. Minor bushwhacking for a few yards to a short, steep, loose descent with minor 3rd class scrambling.

Turn South
34° 12' 55" N
110° 59' 18" W

Swim Hole
34° 12' 19" N
110° 59' 21" W

Haigler

Creek

TRANS LINE

BM
5297

Alderwood
Recreation Site

× 5592

Rim
Tank

0   .5   1 mile

Haiger Creek

A short slot with a couple of tubs. Walls go up 40 to 60 feet, and the bottom is only ten feet wide. The best tub is right in the middle of the slot at the bottom of the descent. It's just the right size for a couple and there is a small lounging rock adjoining it. Also note a gravel pocket the size of a single bed tucked up on the left as you look down canyon. It's shaded by a small sycamore tree and it makes for a really nice place to escape into the shade. Trouble with this tub is that to be more than six feet deep requires a rate of flow which could be a little dangerous.

But nothing compared to the danger this area was famous for at the end of the 19th century. The notorious "Pleasant Valley War" was a feud that made the Hatfields and McCoys look like an ice cream social. Two rival ranching families, the Tewksburys and the Grahams, carried on a range war between 1886 to 1892 that left as many as 50 dead. It finally ended when the last Tewksbury killed the last Graham in Tempe.

Although the hole is clearly known, as evidenced by fire rings upstream, usership does not appear nearly as heavy as other places on this part of Haigler Creek.

Why Bother

Tonto Falls

Given the outstanding features on Tonto Creek, this little cascade on Forest Service 289 just below the state fish hatchery is a yawn.

Horton Creek

A series of really pretty little falls about 1.5 mi from the confluence with Tonto Creek. But their height is only a couple of feet, not enough to produce pools at the bottom.

Fossil Creek (below Irving)

A couple of drive-up spots along Forest Service 502 between the Irving Power Plant and the Child's Power Plant. Possibly worth visiting if you have small children unable to make the hike into the springs. Otherwise too crowded.

Water Wheel

Wade spot in the water next to a campground. 'Nother yawn.

Box Canyon

Too many Yahoos. Here's an idea for an environmental art project. Collect the shards of broken bottles at Box Canyon and arrange them into a large mosaic that reads "No Glass Containers." Install it at the trailhead.

Workman Creek Falls

Water splatters on bare rock. Loads of people, too.

Sheep's Crossing

East Verde ford where four-wheel drive enthusiasts gather to display their shiny vehicles.

Sedona & Flagstaff

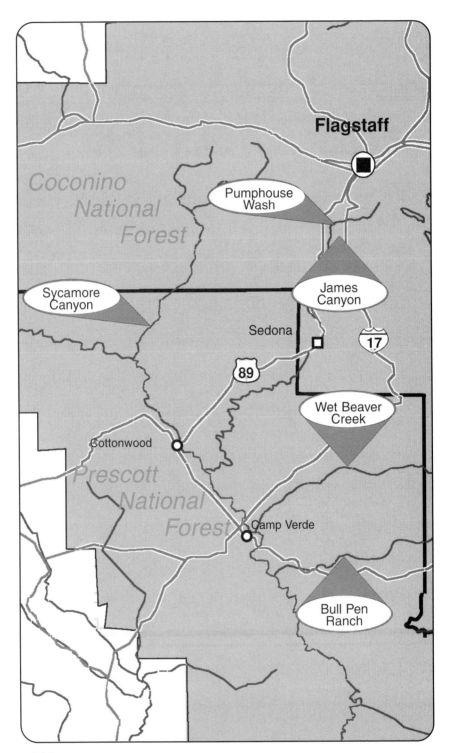

Flagstaff

Coconino
National
Forest

Pumphouse
Wash

Sycamore
Canyon

James
Canyon

Sedona

89

17

Wet Beaver
Creek

Cottonwood

Prescott
National
Forest

Camp Verde

Bull Pen
Ranch

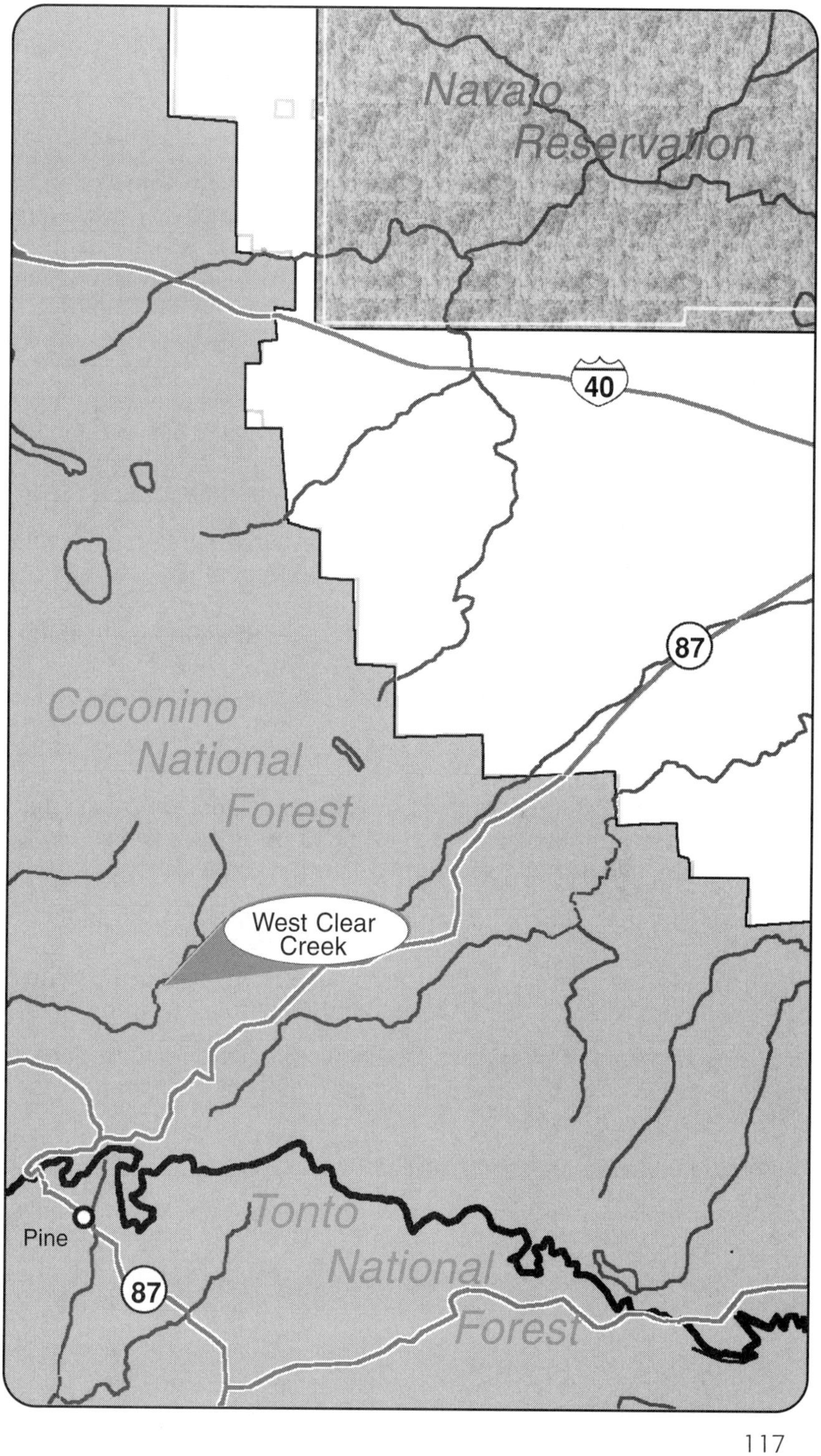

Navajo Reservation

40

87

Coconino
National
Forest

West Clear
Creek

87

Pine

Tonto
National
Forest

The Bikini as a Writing Tool

I've been all over Arizona and Arizona has been all over me.

At first I tried to resist the dust. Ziplock bags were deployed in great numbers. Stuff sacks were double checked to ensure they were closed and I ran through moist towelettes faster than a family with twins.

Then I surrendered and was happier for it.

In the morning I rinsed my coffee cup with grit; in the evening I filled my sleeping bag with sand. I mixed mud in my chewing tobacco and loaded my running shorts with gravel. It paid off, too. I got a letter from the Smithsonian saying that the museum was planning a special exhibit on dirt and they wanted me to curate it.

The centerpiece would be the Research Vessel, my faithful Toyota truck. Before it became a rolling demonstration of effluvia, flotsam, dust and detritus, it was a carefully engineered tool for travel and designed along the aesthetic expressed by French author and aviator Eugene St. Exupery. The perfect design, he said, is one in which nothing can be added or removed.

The bed of a Toyota Tacoma is six feet long. I'm 5'11" and 7/8. Perfect, no wasted space. I slid the plywood sleeping pallet in and noticed that the space it occupied between the wheel wells was the exact dimensions of my Bokara prayer rug, a beautifully woven work of wool that's followed me everywhere since college.

The pattern of a prayer rug is fashioned to represent the center aisle of a mosque. Nomadic people of the Middle East carry one so that no matter where they are in their wanderings, they can lay the rug down with the nave facing Mecca and recite their prayers.

I sort of adopted the practice. Each evening I point my truck east before I shut the engine off and crawl into the back. Apparently, the spiritual approach worked.

Now the blonde in the black bikini.

She wasn't result of prayer, not mine anyway. She's my cousin's wife. They live in Phoenix and agreed to visit one of these swimming holes for some pictures. In addition to the photo, I got an invitation to spend the weekend at her mother's fabulous home on Camelback Mountain.

"There's plenty of room in the guest house," she said, "and

Playboy's lingerie magazine is doing a photo shoot there Saturday."

The model arrived before the rest of the crew. She was a 24-year-old Yugoslavian with long, straight hair the color of cherry Coke. Her name was Milanka.

She claimed degrees in international business and German. She spoke French and some Italian, but the way I could tell she was intelligent was that she laughed at my jokes.

Understand that since I started researching the guide book many months earlier, the only thing in my lap was a steering wheel. Earlier that morning, the Labrador Retriever that lives here woke me up and I realized how long it's been since I felt heavy breathing in the bed next to me.

Now there's this whole THING going on upstairs in the bedroom.

The production eventually moved to the pool deck. While they set up, Milanka was topless except for a black shirt so sheer you could read the morning paper through it. I was talking to her from the other side of the breakfast island, making solid, solid eye contact.

We talked about the political situation in the Balkans, but before we could get to the topic of Serbian nationalism and Kosovo crisis, she was outside in a thong bikini that made her buttocks look like twin sisters to the moon.

Afterward, when they were packing things up, I heard her talking to the hostess about exercise routines.

"I love to swim," she said, "to swim in the ocean and the rivers. My friends, my husband they sit on the beach and they say, 'look at her go.'"

I bolted for my truck. I was still breathing heavily when I gave her the business card I snatched off the front seat. "Have you got a sister?"

"Yes. She lives in Yugoslavia."

"I'm available to relocate."

I gave her my business card. We all said good-bye and shook hands. "Oooh. Nice firm handshake," she told me.

"It should be," I said. "I've been trying to keep a grip all day."

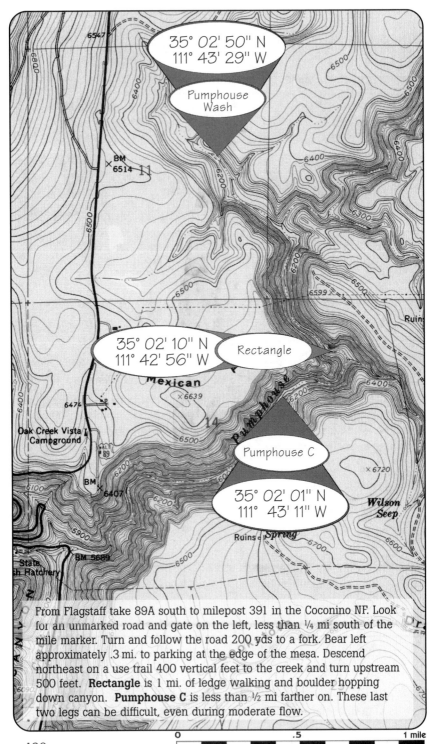

35° 02' 50" N
111° 43' 29" W

Pumphouse Wash

35° 02' 10" N
111° 42' 56" W

Rectangle

Pumphouse C

35° 02' 01" N
111° 43' 11" W

From Flagstaff take 89A south to milepost 391 in the Coconino NF. Look for an unmarked road and gate on the left, less than ¼ mi south of the mile marker. Turn and follow the road 200 yds to a fork. Bear left approximately .3 mi. to parking at the edge of the mesa. Descend northeast on a use trail 400 vertical feet to the creek and turn upstream 500 feet. **Rectangle** is 1 mi. of ledge walking and boulder hopping down canyon. **Pumphouse C** is less than ½ mi farther on. These last two legs can be difficult, even during moderate flow.

0   .5   1 mile

Pumphouse Wash

In a place as crowded as Oak Creek Canyon you have to go pretty high up the watershed to leave the riffraff behind. Pumphouse Wash drains the top of the canyon. At 6000 feet elevation this hole is at the practical cutoff for swimming holes considered warm enough to be comfortable. But it's a near classic and to leave out this and the two other places featured on the following pages would be a glaring omission.

The big show is crescent-shaped and about 40 feet wide. Water arrives through a rifle-notch channel cut deep into the basalt and over a fall about 10 feet high. The rock has big, blocky fractures. On the right as you look upstream it's loose and brushy. Action is on the left wall. It's around 40 feet high with good seating and a ledge at 20 feet that may be jumpable, but I wasn't able to confirm this. Seating at the water is sparse, mostly cobble with a couple of sofa-sized boulders. Note: If the water is high enough to cover the lounging rocks, chances are good that it will be too cold to jump in without suffering an embarrassing temporary physical affect. (Guys, you know what I'm talking about.)

Expectation of privacy is fair. You'll find better privacy about one-half mile farther down where a wall running southwest creates a basin about 70 feet long. There's a rope swing attached to a spruce tree, but it looked more like a place to pass through than a destination.

Hell's Gate

Rectangle

Gorgeous place to pull off your clothes. The sides of the pool are parallel, creating a nearly perfect rectangle, around six feet deep. Water enters across a broad slab, one that must make a dandy slide on a hot day in August. Rocks stretch out on both sides of the pool, adding further to the charming appearance. At the optimum water level, these ledges will be around one foot above the surface so you can dangle your legs in the cool water while you work on that poem you've been meaning to write.

Not in a literary mood? There's enough seating on the left to have a party. A tremendous sense of enclosure aided by a beautiful, blank sandstone wall on the right as you look upstream. Even though this part of the canyon faces west, the walls keep the afternoon sun from becoming too intrusive. And in truth, it makes the water just a little too cold. Be prepared.

You reach here by starting downstream from the spot reviewed on the preceding page. It's more than a mile, twisting and turning in a southerly direction before the canyon hooks to the east and delivers you immediately to the top of the hole.

Tonto Creek (p. 105)

Martini Glass

A narrow trough points to a fan-shaped pool about 25 feet wide. The main chamber is six to ten feet deep where part of the stone has been scooped by spring runoff from Flagstaff and environs. It's at the bottom of a narrow canyon where run off has etched a thin line in the rock such that you can get in the water and start swimming 100 feet before you even get to the fat part of the hole. The surrounding ledges are ten and fifteen feet above the water and give out over what should be a deep part of the pool.

Seating at the water level is on uneven, medium-sized boulders that nevertheless are set at a nice angle facing the pool. There's plenty of lounge area on nice flat terraces above. On the right the stone is so even and flat that it looks like it was smoothed out with a concrete trowel. Deep shade, too. Problem is that it's difficult to get back to the ledges once you jump in the water. Since the rock is steeply undercut and leaves no footing at water level, you have to walk around.

Not much evidence of usership. That's partly because the approach is a little tricky. From the hole reviewed on the previous page, you continue southeast down the canyon for a couple of hundred yards to where it turns southwest. There, the water cuts into a slick rock channel forty feet deep and just six feet wide in places. The best way past is on the ledge above the narrows to the east. It's one quarter mile downstream from there.

35° 03' 08" N
111° 41' 01" W
Parking

35° 03' 00" N
111° 42' 17" W
James Canyon

35° 02' 49" N
111° 41' 29" W
Crossing

From Flagstaff drive south on I-17 through the Coconino NF to the Kelly Canyon exit and turn west to park on the access road. Head south along a dirt road and power line paralleling the highway for .6 mi to the head of the canyon. Walk less than ½ mi with the canyon on your left then locate the crossing. Some route finding might be req'd. You can turn upstream from here to visit some upper pools or continue 1 mi downstream for the main attraction.

James Canyon

A secret place in plain view. The entrance to the canyon is less than one mile from an Interstate, yet very little visited. It's a short canyon, narrow and around 300 feet deep with at least a couple of places worth checking out. Shortly after turning onto the rim of the canyon you pass some pools and tubs, but the main feature is more than one mile farther down where a rifle-sight notch discharges into a wide hole with a steep headwall and brushy sides.

The diameter of the pool is more than 40 feet wide. Depth was difficult to gauge since, at the time it was reviewed, monsoon rain had filled the canyon with muddy water. When it's filled with late-season snow melt though, the color and clarity should be excellent. It will be cold, though. The elevation is right at the upper limit for swimming holes considered warm enough to be enjoyable.

You reach this lower hole by crossing the canyon at the indicated spot and continuing downstream on the south side. The trail is less discernable, sometimes in the streambed, sometimes on the left bank until you reach the pour-off. There will be a rappel sling on an old log. Alternately you can climb steeply to the left through moderate brush and duff, then work your way down to the creek bed via a forested gully.

For the upper pools, simply double back upstream from the crossing and negotiate about 50 feet of water-filled creek.

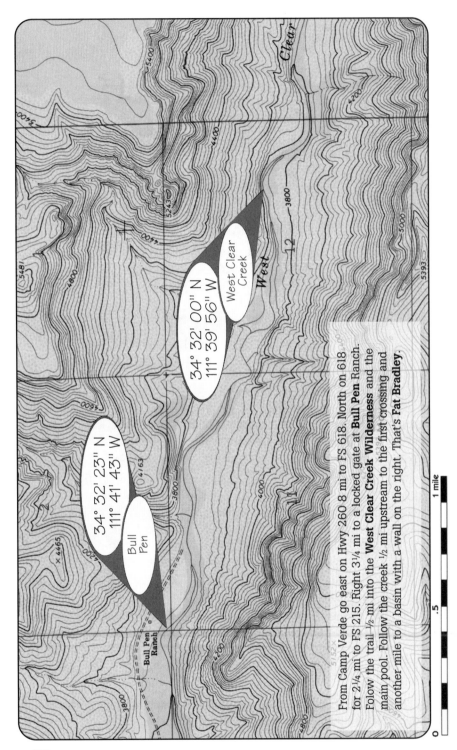

34° 32' 23" N
111° 41' 43" W

Bull Pen

34° 32' 00" N
111° 39' 56" W

West Clear Creek

From Camp Verde go east on Hwy 260 8 mi to FS 618. North on 618
for 2¼ mi to FS 215. Right 3¼ mi to a locked gate at **Bull Pen** Ranch.
Folow the trail ½ mi into the **West Clear Creek Wilderness** and the
main pool. Follow the creek ½ mi upstream to the first crossing and
another mile to a basin with a wall on the right. That's **Fat Bradley**.

0   .5   1 mile

Bull Pen

Weekday Classic. Bull Pen gets overrun on weekends because it's so accessible and so much fun. The main pool is at least 60 feet wide with a really nice sand beach that slopes right into the water. Opposite the beach is a rock wall that acts as the dive platform, with ledges at 9, 18 and 25 feet. Attached above it is a rope swing, which is the real reason people come here—big air.

Katelyn Baker, a Camp Verde resident and rope swing regular, gives some tips. She recommends that you dry your hands off before grabbing the rope. Also, since the rope hangs a good six feet beyond the ledge, you need to use a stick to snag it and pull it toward you. Most important, don't swing straight out. You get lots more clearance if you let the rope carry you out in a circle.

"It takes less energy to swing in a circle," Baker said. "You just time the release when you reach the most distant point on the circle."

For a demonstration of her skill, see the feature photo on the following page.

The shade, beach and accessibility make this a good kid spot. Room for three or four groups, although there is likely to be many more than that on a weekend. Lots of bozos and yahoos, although I didn't see any broken glass. A good sign.

Bull Pen

Fat Bradley

Many pools above Bull Pen, none as spectacular, but all with better privacy. Fat Bradley forms where the creek bends against a rock wall. The ledge above the water is four to seven feet and suitable for stepping off into the sliver of deep water along the wall. Most of the rest of the pool is filled with gravel and even some mud at the fringes. Best recommendation is to stick close to the wall so as not to stir the bottom up.

Vegetation is dense all around the pool. More than a wrap around skirt of green, actually it's a tangle of lesser plant life. But since this lower end of West Clear Creek gets visited frequently, the trail in involves only moderate brush busting. Creek crossings are usually no more than knee-deep. Cairns mark each crossing.

Truthfully, I was disinclined to review either of these spots on lower West Clear Creek. The stream gradient is low and visitorship high. But I include them in the interest of serving a broader public. If you're recovering from knee surgery or you're a pack-a-day smoker, lower West Clear Creek might suit you. One note: if you puff, you have to bring a plastic bag or something to put your butts into. They're too many Marlboro skeletons and Winston stumps around from inconsiderate smokers.

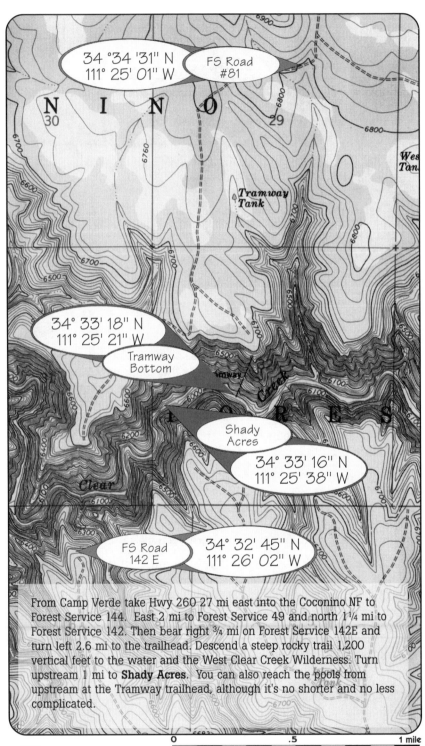

34°34'31" N
111° 25' 01" W

FS Road #81

34° 33' 18" N
111° 25' 21" W

Tramway Bottom

Shady Acres

34° 33' 16" N
111° 25' 38" W

FS Road 142 E

34° 32' 45" N
111° 26' 02" W

Tramway Tank

Clear

Creek

From Camp Verde take Hwy 260 27 mi east into the Coconino NF to Forest Service 144. East 2 mi to Forest Service 49 and north 1¼ mi to Forest Service 142. Then bear right ¾ mi on Forest Service 142E and turn left 2.6 mi to the trailhead. Descend a steep rocky trail 1,200 vertical feet to the water and the West Clear Creek Wilderness. Turn upstream 1 mi to **Shady Acres**. You can also reach the pools from upstream at the Tramway trailhead, although it's no shorter and no less complicated.

0   .5   1 mile

Shady Acres

West Clear Creek zigzags between sheer walls that are 100 feet high and more. It's not a really tight canyon. Walls alternate with steep wooded slopes and side canyons. In between is a riverbed filled with small cobble and gravel. The pools occur in places where the water piles up against one of these walls to create long, narrow pools accompanied by a broad terrace of grass and gravel.

Both are similar: arcs of green, 90 feet long, that lie against a vertical rock face 150 feet high. The walls above are mottled green from moss and lichen growing there as well as on the camping benches above. Depth during the season is around five feet.

There is another series of pools at the bottom of the trail. No jumps. No plunge pools or anything like that. Depth will be six to eight feet at best. More than anything, it's a good hot weather spot. Morning exposure chases away the chill, then the sun ducks behind a wall that runs southeast to northwest and it will stay cool and shady. Trees on the camping bench above improve shade even more.

On a weekend you'll find one dozen people or more, many of them doing car shuttle hikes through the canyon. Privacy is only fair. The other drawback is the muddy bottom, probably due to a fire above the creek in 1996.

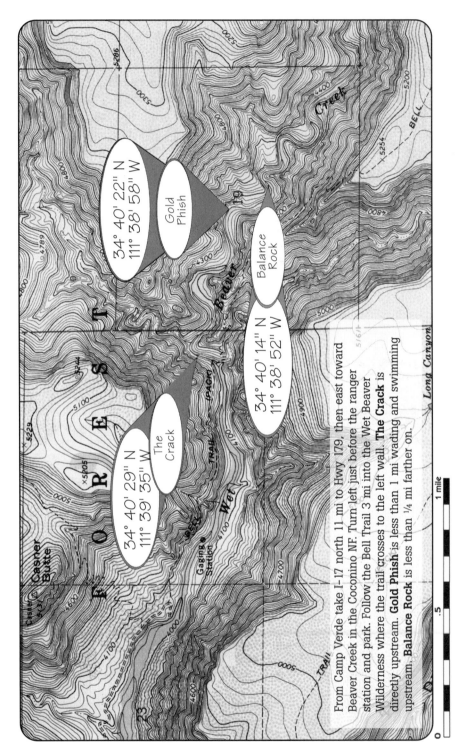

34° 40' 22" N
111° 38' 58" W

Gold Phish

34° 40' 29" N
111° 39' 35" W

The Crack

Balance Rock

34° 40' 14" N
111° 38' 52" W

From Camp Verde take I-17 north 11 mi to Hwy 179, then east toward Beaver Creek in the Coconino NF. Turn left just before the ranger station and park. Follow the Bell Trail 3 mi into the Wet Beaver Wilderness where the trail crosses to the left wall. **The Crack** is directly upstream. **Gold Phish** is less than 1 mi wading and swimming upstream. **Balance Rock** is less than ¼ mi farther on.

.5   1 mile

The Crack

A combination of rock and water that could make a poet out of a plowman. The Wet Beaver Wilderness collects runoff from between Apache Maid and Oak Hill, then turns it into a lyrical combination of sandstone and water. Brick red terraces the size of tennis courts lead down to a channel 20 feet wide and 60 feet long. The most dramatic spot is a rock wedge jutting into the flow that produces a triangular diving ledge leaning over deep water.

The trail to the hole runs from west to east, such that if you're headed out in the morning and returning in the evening, you'll be squinting both directions. Whichever direction, take a break from the hike to turn around and look at the ground you've covered and you'll find the mesas illuminated by a heartbreaking light. Lots of wind-scarred juniper with dead, cracked branches in contrasty light. They look like they're auditioning for an Ansel Adams photo.

There's a good kiddie pool along the Weir Trail, flat pools with cobble impoundments and easy entry with slow water about 600 feet below a gauging station. A good place to take baby so they won't tip over and roll down the hill.

During the weekend there may be as many as 20 cars at the trailhead, and that's not counting people at the campground. Many users spread out along the creek or follow the popular pack trail up to the mesa, but be prepared for neighbors when you visit The Crack.

The Crack

Gold Phish

A short narrows produces a slot pool 80 feet by 20 feet. Best use is lap swimming and lounging. It's not deep in the center, but at the corners eddies create deep water. The hole faces due north, it's open and sunny with broken vertical walls that rise 70 feet on the west side and about half that on the east. Jumps are seven to ten feet above the western alcove, but you have to work to get there. The slab leading from the water up to the ledge is at a steep angle.

If you visit in May or June look for fish in spawning coloration. One species, the Desert Mountain Sucker can look almost like goldfish. Scott Reger, a fish biologist for the department of Game and Fish said that in some cases the whole lower half of the body turns color.

"Lots of fish do that sort of seasonal advertising. They can't go buy Maybelline, so they have to do it themselves. But in the case of fish, it's mostly the males that change color."

There is a supreme ledge on the east side. About 15 feet above the water. Not for diving, but for lounging. It's close to 100 square feet with a corresponding overhang that makes a canopy, creating a great place to survey swallows hunting insects. The catch is you need to be able to make a couple of rock climbing moves to get there. Try it. Otherwise use a deeply shaded pocket of cobbles at the top of the pool, just to the left of the cascade.

Balance Rock

A big ol' balanced rock sits right at the center of a horseshoe shaped pool. It's around 70 feet in circumference with a mondo, fatty deep end at the apex of the horseshoe. The water is plenty deep for diving. It's clear, green and begging you to jump. The pool is formed by a finger of rock that forces the bend in the creek. The balanced rock is right at the tip of the finger, capping a classic, classic swimming hole.

Although barely visited now, it's been popular in years past, several hundred years past. Indian ruins are nestled in a small overhang near the hole. If you want to examine it, do so from a distance. There's been significant damage to archeological sites in the canyon. Destruction has been particularly bad in the past few years, officials say.

From a user's standpoint, the only negative about this spot is that there is no really good place to sit. About the only option is on the right at the top of the hole. It's an area covered with grass that gives out onto some broad submerged slabs. Use care entering and exiting and be careful not to trample the grass.

Plenty of wading and some swimming between here and the trailhead. Lots of slippery rocks, too. Bring a walking stick and make it a sturdy one.

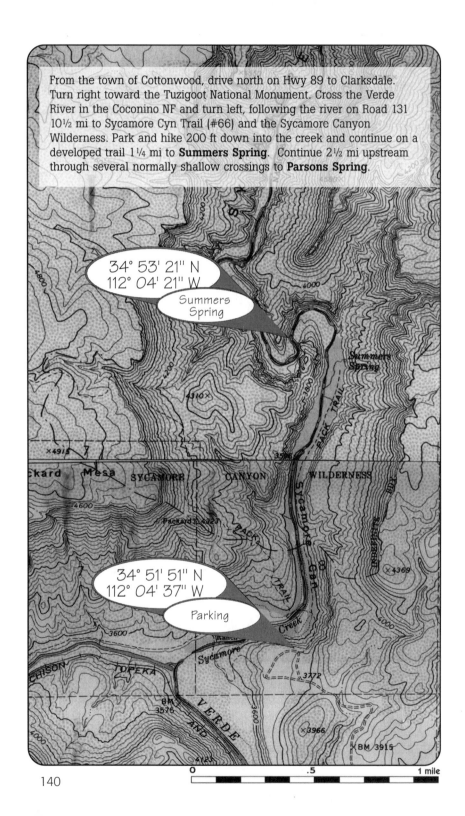

From the town of Cottonwood, drive north on Hwy 89 to Clarksdale. Turn right toward the Tuzigoot National Monument. Cross the Verde River in the Coconino NF and turn left, following the river on Road 131 10½ mi to Sycamore Cyn Trail (#66) and the Sycamore Canyon Wilderness. Park and hike 200 ft down into the creek and continue on a developed trail 1¼ mi to **Summers Spring**. Continue 2½ mi upstream through several normally shallow crossings to **Parsons Spring**.

34° 53' 21" N
112° 04' 21" W

Summers Spring

34° 51' 51" N
112° 04' 37" W

Parking

0   .5   1 mile

Sycamore Canyon

The first good swimming hole occurs just after Summers Spring. You'll notice the trail turns to the west as you head upstream. On the left is a north-south ridge about 200 feet high which forces a hairpin turn in the creek. On the western side of the ridge the water has created a hole deep enough for submarine races. Wide and long, too. It spans 50 feet and stretches for nearly 250 feet in some places.

Look for a couple of diving ledges at six feet and at 15 feet on a terrace opposite the trail. There's tremendous, if not inconvenient seating on the terrace. Trailside, there's sand and cobble. Scattered shade, but mostly lots of sky. You can duck into willows for comfort from the heat. Also look for sand benches to the west and north-west.

Just under one mile upstream is a set of west-facing limestone ledges. Below is a beautiful hole, 100 feet long and 30 feet wide. Sand and cobble in the bottom. Gorgeous place. You'll find it a couple of hundred yards above where the canyon dog legs to the east. Parsons Springs is 1 1/4 miles farther up the canyon. Above the spring, the amount of water in the canyon diminishes considerably.

Why Bother

Lower West Fork Oak Creek
All the twists and turns in the canyon west of Alt 89 make it seem like there should be some deep pools. But I went five miles west, up the canyon and didn't find anything deep enough.

Slide Rock
Slide Rock Campground 8 miles north of Sedona. So many people it regularly gets shut down because the fecal coliform bacteria gets too high. Yuk!

Grasshopper Point
Oak Creek, just over ½ mile north of the Midgley Bridge on Alt 89 right next to the road. Major cliff diving spot. Crowds with beer coolers.

Colorado River Basin

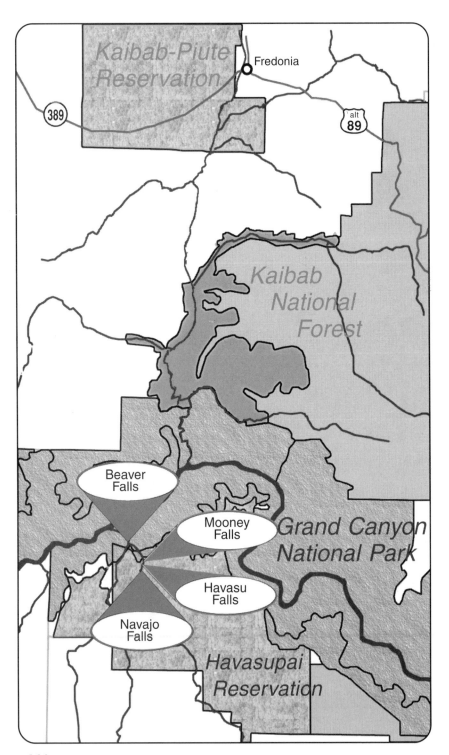

Kaibab-Piute
Reservation

Fredonia

389

alt
89

Kaibab
National
Forest

Beaver
Falls

Mooney
Falls

Grand Canyon
National Park

Havasu
Falls

Navajo
Falls

Havasupai
Reservation

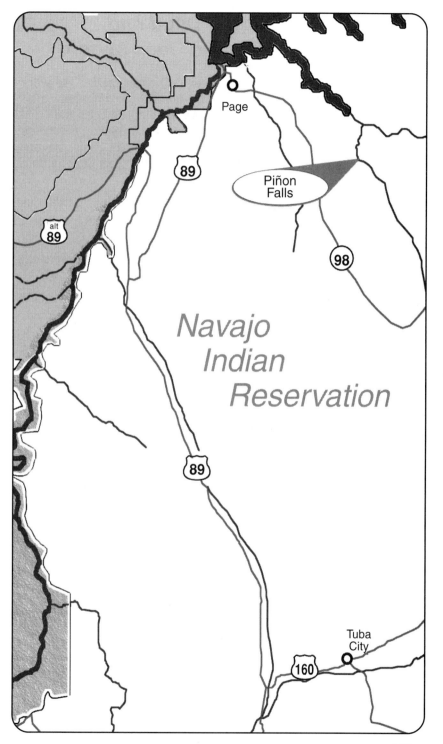

Page

89

alt
89

Piñon
Falls

98

*Navajo
Indian
Reservation*

89

Tuba
City

160

Castañeda is Dead and I'm Not Feeling too Good Myself

I'd been hiking for about an hour with Thomas Yazzie. We were descending toward Lake Powell and the flooded canyon where his family and generations of Navajos before them raised corn and sheep. The weather was hot and we talked about plants. He showed me locoweed and told me a little about sheep ranching and growing up on the Colorado River before completion of the Glen Canyon dam in 1963.

"Me and my cousins spent so much time in the river that we bled. That's hard water and the minerals dry your skin, but we just kept on."

One day at the river, he thinks he must have been five years old, he said that he saw a white man for the first time.

"We saw him paddling down the river and we hid in the bushes so he wouldn't see us," Thomas laughed. "Sometimes planes would fly over. We called them flying cars."

In addition to corn, the family raised vegetables, like carrots for mutton stew. They even had an orchard and for fresh water, they used a spring where water shot straight out of the ground in a column 5-feet tall.

His dad constructed the trail down to the canyon with a pick and shovel. He's buried on the mesa, in a lone plot.

Thomas isn't the genuine article, not someone living the traditional life he was telling me about. He's a welder at a coalmine. From what I can tell, he's like lots of the Navajos here, late model pick-ups, new houses, boats — and a union wage buys lots of powerboat. It's a middle-class success story, yet Thomas exchanged his Mormon credentials for a federal license to use peyote and a return to traditional beliefs.

"The Navajo believe everything from the ground up is the father and everything below is the mother. The Morning Prayer is to the father in the east. Our children, when we send them to bed, we say grandfather will come wake you up in the morning."

Sacred springs, the peyote ceremony, what color north is. The man had credibility. He even told me how to avoid bad luck if a coyote crosses your path. Answer: corn pollen. But he was repeating himself. Badly. After an hour he refereed to something for what must have been the one-hundredth time as "from the Earth."

Granted, we're surrounded by dramatic landscape, corkscrew canyons 1,000 feet deep, buttes, mesas...you name it...lots of room for the "from the Earth" reference. But he applied it to everything, including at one point, his 3/4-ton Chevy with the 300-gallon water tank in the bed. His Chevy was from the Earth.

"A truck is not the sky. It's not the wind or sun. A truck is a place I can get in and feel comfortable. It's the mother. Plus this truck brings water. It's from the Earth."

Ok, suppose he's right. And nevermind that he helps supply coal to a nearby generating plant described as the dirtiest in the state. Forget that. I liked the guy. So what if his doctrine wasn't in perfect order?

But while we were talking, he opened the seal on a gallon jug of water and dropped the plastic strip on the ground between us.

What should I do?

His people have been worshiping these mountains and rivers for generations. I've been a white, liberal environmentalist for about 10 years. I'd been in the area less than 24-hours, whereas the Yazzie family was connected to this canyon by blood, sweat and now a little blue strip of plastic 3-inches long.

If he were a white man, I'd have laid into him about the litter or at least handed it back to him, saying, "Excuse me, I think you dropped this." But I was off balance, so I waited until he wasn't watching, discretely retrieved the litter and put it in my pocket.

"That spring was real sacred to us," he continued. "When you walked up to it, the pressure would decrease and the fountain would get lower the closer you got. If you ran up to the spring real fast, the water would go down right away. If you crawled up to it, the pressure would decrease real slow.

"Our old corral is under 150 feet of water. The spring is under about 75 feet," he said. "I go out there in my boat and look down sometimes. I guess it's still running."

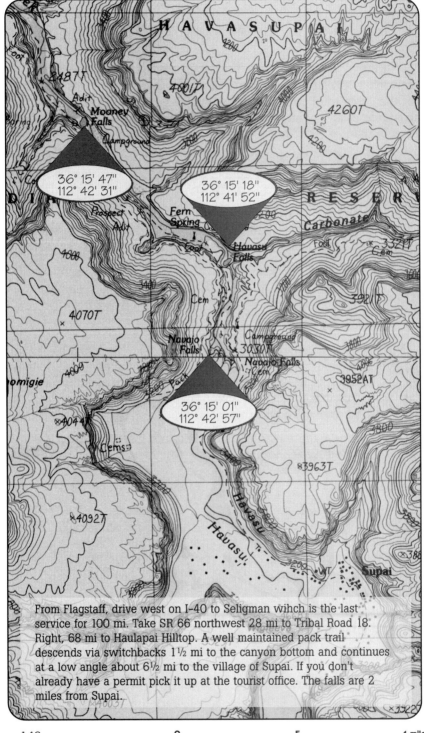

36° 15' 47"
112° 42' 31"

36° 15' 18"
112° 41' 52"

36° 15' 01"
112° 42' 57"

From Flagstaff, drive west on I-40 to Seligman wihch is the last service for 100 mi. Take SR 66 northwest 28 mi to Tribal Road 18. Right, 68 mi to Haulapai Hilltop. A well maintained pack trail descends via switchbacks 1½ mi to the canyon bottom and continues at a low angle about 6½ mi to the village of Supai. If you don't already have a permit pick it up at the tourist office. The falls are 2 miles from Supai.

0   .5   1 mile

Havasu Falls

A divine blue crystal, but one you'll have to share with a couple of hundred strangers. The popularity of Havasu Falls, and the rest of the canyon, exceeds the level of privacy established for this book. Nevertheless, there's no way to exclude so rare a beauty.

Caribbean-blue water roars from a spring just above the village of Supai at 180,000 gallons a minute and at a constant temperature of 72 degrees. It rolls down the canyon and spills over a fall, 106 feet high. Minerals dissolved from the limestone give the water its color and produce the travertine deposits forming the 100-foot-wide main pool as well as the handful of other pools below.

This is in the Havasupai Reservation, so permits are required. Make reservations early. Temperature regularly tops the century mark so bring plenty of water. This isn't a practical day trip unless you are a hard-core trail runner. No ground fires, so you have to bring a stove. If you forget something, supplies are available at the store in town, although you'll pay more.

For permits and other information contact:

Havasupai Tourist Enterprize,
Supai, AZ 86435
(520) 448-2141

Havasu Falls

Navajo Falls

The runt of the litter. Navajo Falls is dwarfed by its downstream cousins. The pool is nice sized, though. Around 70 feet on the main axis and deep enough for diving, although there isn't anything to dive from. Instead of rocks, the pool is surrounded by dense vegetation. Consequently, the seating is very limited. But on the other hand, visitorship is relatively low. The trail to Havasu Fall goes past Navajo, but it's on the other side of the canyon and screened from view. To reach it, you'll have to cross about one-quarter mile below and turn back up canyon. Signs make it easy to find.

Havasupai means "people of the blue green-waters." They say this is the most isolated reservation in the country. There's no road, only a pack trail that descends nine miles and 2,000 vertical feet to the village of Supai. Historically, it's not a year-round village. The Havasupai people farmed the canyon, but spent much of the year hunting and trading on the plateau with only a contingent left behind to tend the crops. That changed in the 19th Century, when settlers forced the tribe into the canyon permanently.

Now, teams of one dozen pack animals do the daily supply, carrying more than a ton of goods into the village of 350 people. Mail, too. And in the most isolated village in the country they still get junk mail.

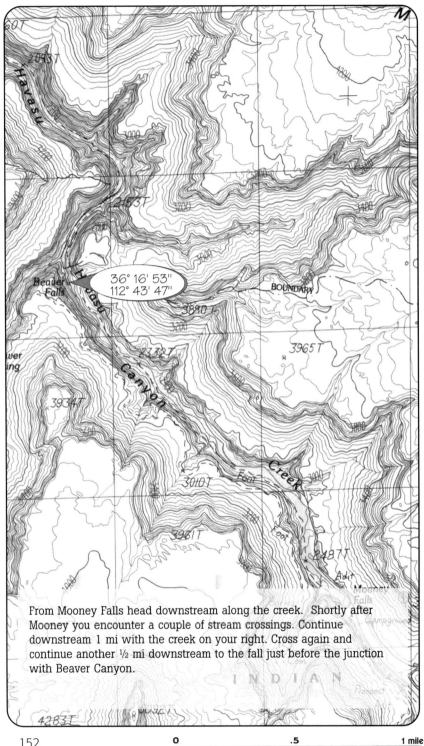

36° 16' 53"
112° 43' 47"

From Mooney Falls head downstream along the creek. Shortly after Mooney you encounter a couple of stream crossings. Continue downstream 1 mi with the creek on your right. Cross again and continue another ½ mi downstream to the fall just before the junction with Beaver Canyon.

0   .5   1 mile

Beaver Falls

Really interesting travertine deposits with three or more swim-mable pools stretching between the fall and the mouth of Beaver Canyon to the west. The drawback I observed was that the banks are either crumbling rock or exasperating brush. One might think that by the time you reach this part of the canyon two miles below Mooney Falls you would find a good expectation of privacy. While it's true Beaver Falls gets fewer visitors from above, it's close enough to the Grand Canyon (3 miles) that it attracts rafters doing day hikes upstream.

Kids from Supai sometimes come here to escape the crowds. During the school year though it's an adults only village. Children are sent to boarding schools or to live with relatives in cities where they can attend classes.

"The first time they took me I felt like I was being kidnapped, said Roland Manakaja, natural resources director for tribe. "I thought we were just going for a bus ride. At the end of the school year, when the bus was coming to take us home, we'd stay up all night waiting to see if we were really going back."

If you want to visit Beaver Falls you will definitely need to overnight at the campground unless you think you might value the experience of shuffling back up the grade by head lamp after 30 miles and 3,000 vertical feet.

Mooney Falls

Mooney Falls

Two-hundred feet high. It's even taller than Niagra Falls. You can't get closer than 30 feet from the fall without being blasted backward by the force of the water. Major floods in 1990, 1993, 1997 blew out most of the travertine deposits that created pools more than 20 feet deep. After 1993 you could walk up to the falls and touch them. But they have regenerated nicely since then. The pool at the bottom of Mooney is about the same size as the main tank at Havasu, although it doesn't have as many associated pools downstream.

The campground is strung out between Havasu and Mooney Falls. When I visited, it seemed underdeveloped for the number of over-night guests permitted. Sanitary facilities were third world, but officials said they are studying different systems and hope to have eight or more composting toilets to improve service.

After negotiating the campground, the trail descends to Mooney Falls through two low tunnels and a series of steps and ladders cut into the rock. Primitive hand rails should give some confidence to those afraid of heights.

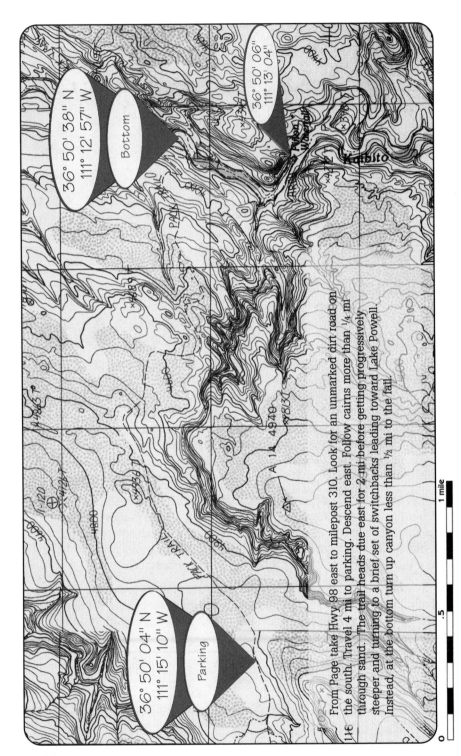

From Page take Hwy 98 east to milepost 310. Look for an unmarked dirt road on the south. Travel 4 mi to parking. Descend east. Follow cairns more than ¼ mi through sand. The trail heads due east for 2 mi before getting progressively steeper and turning to a brief set of switchbacks leading toward Lake Powell. Instead, at the bottom turn up canyon less than ½ mi to the fall.

36° 50' 04" N
111° 15' 10" W
Parking

36° 50' 38" N
111° 12' 57" W
Bottom

36° 50' 06" N
111° 13' 04" W

Kaibito

0   .5   1 mile

Piñon Falls

Favorite activities include standing in a natural stone chamber and being showered with water from the Rainbow Plateau. Kaibito Creek produces Baroque shapes in Navajo Sandstone, right at a boundary with some harder limestone. The canyon floor above is flat and level enough that you could bring a Frisbee to toss around. Then the water pours off the limestone in a short, broad arc that erodes the softer stone below.

There might be dozens of thin rivulets comprising a cascade 30 feet wide, but only a couple of feet high. The water accelerates, carving countless troughs and curves before taking a 12-foot plunge. Individual streams of water tumble together into a collection of head-high chambers. There's even an arch you can walk through.

During the summer season, the water won't be more than waist deep, except after storms when it will be dark and gritty anyway. It's no more than a three mile hike up from the lake, so best visit early in the season, when the lake is still low, thus the hike for boaters is longer.

It's a long trip from above. At least three hours along faint trails with several opportunities for wrong turns. When the arm of the lake comes into view, look for descending switchbacks and at the bottom turn up canyon.

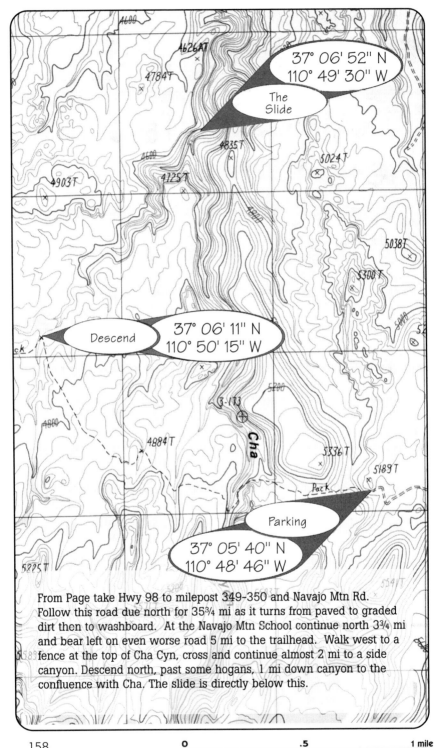

37° 06' 52" N
110° 49' 30" W

The Slide

4626AT

4784T

4835T

5024T

4600

4125T

4903T

5038T

5300 T

37° 06' 11" N
110° 50' 15" W

Descend

ck

4800

G-173

Cha

4884T

5336 T

5189T

Pack

Parking

37° 05' 40" N
110° 48' 46" W

5225T

5541T

From Page take Hwy 98 to milepost 349-350 and Navajo Mtn Rd.
Follow this road due north for 35¾ mi as it turns from paved to graded
dirt then to washboard. At the Navajo Mtn School continue north 3¾ mi
and bear left on even worse road 5 mi to the trailhead. Walk west to a
fence at the top of Cha Cyn, cross and continue almost 2 mi to a side
canyon. Descend north, past some hogans, 1 mi down canyon to the
confluence with Cha. The slide is directly below this.

0   .5   1 mile

Cha Canyon

Slot pools that aren't going to change your life, but you'll enjoy an excellent expectation of privacy. The destination is The Slide, a 20-foot ride with a four foot free fall at the end. The pool itself is really deep. Be advised, steep sides mean getting out once you're in can be difficult. Twenty feet of rope would be helpful, but there's no technical climbing required.

Between the descent and the destination are a couple of pots, one more than 40 feet wide and eight feet deep in the center. It's shaped like a drinking gourd and deep along "handle" where water comes in. Jumps on the left.

Below the pot, route finding gets difficult. A deep slot with a square limestone chock stone hinders progress, then the slope walls out below. You cross loose slabs on the right to a small riparian area. Cross gingerly, foot print to foot print, to avoid damaging this fragile pocket of green in the desert. Once through the vegetation, resume the slope on the right side briefly before descending to The Slide.

Note: The drive in is long and rough. Also, hiking permits are required. They are $5 and available at the Navajo Nation Parks and Recreation office way over in Window Rock, or by mail at:

P.O. Box 9000
Window Rock, AZ 86515
(520) 871-6647 or 7307

Why Bother

Black Hole
Brilliant hike, but water temperature is 52 degrees in summer.

Butterfly Canyon
A fall right at the end of the canyon by the lake, but it's a very small watershed. Season is too short.

Tapeats Creek
Tapeats, at least below Thunder River, has too many rapids and rocks.

Deer Creek Falls
Water shoots out of a cliff and meanders through a valley of cottonwoods then into the Colorado River. No swimming holes and lots of rafters.

Zion National Park & the Virgin River

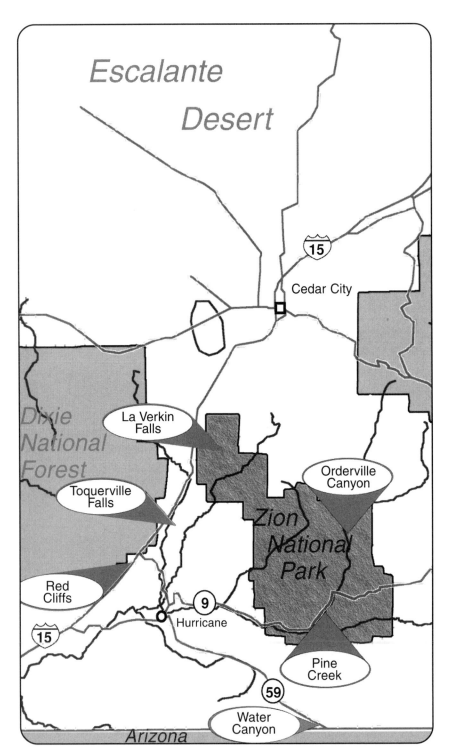

Escalante
Desert

15

Cedar City

Dixie
National
Forest

La Verkin
Falls

Orderville
Canyon

Toquerville
Falls

Zion
National
Park

Red
Cliffs

15

9

Hurricane

Pine
Creek

59

Water
Canyon

Arizona

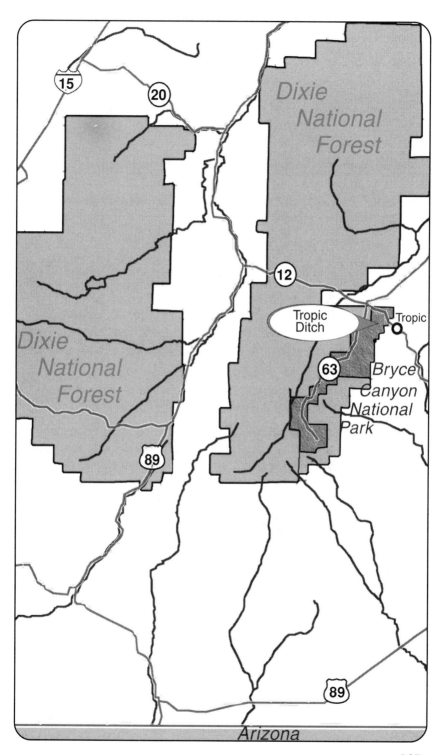

Why BYU Has Such a Good Hoop Squad

I was feeling worn out and figured I ought to get a motel room, shower and check e-mail. Well, I forgot to ask the nice lady at the front desk if they have modular jacks in the rooms.

They don't. Their phones are hard wired, so after my shower I took my computer into the office to see if I could plug into a phone jack there. The nice lady didn't know, but she said she would call her husband.

He clipped me in and we talked about the area. After he finished the obligatory stuff about whose great, great grandfather settled what, he told me about the yearly softball game.

It happened each Memorial Day down in the river bottom. Two rural towns coming together for their annual party. Imagine the picnic baskets. Think of the pies! And all the young people looking one another over. It was truly an event. There were horse races, too.

"That's how most of the fist fights started," the nice lady commented.

The husband recalled how in elementary school his class was recruited into a soil conservation project to plant non-native species like tamarisk. The trees spread down the river and turned sandbars broad enough for a summer softball game into a bushwhack nightmare. You couldn't find a softball if you dropped it on your toe.

Before long we got from tamarisk to another exotic species, the Book of Mormon. I'm intrigued by the Mormon belief that Jesus visited America and their conviction that the U.S Constitution is a divinely inspired document. So I ask questions.

I'm careful to explain that I'm only interested in the Latter Day Saints in as much as I enjoy learning about Americans and their beliefs. But when I told this man that I once read The Bible as a literary exercise, he just assumed he could go deep.

Almost five hours later, I was crawling into bed at 1 a.m. after listening to this man declare his spiritual self so completely that the next morning when he gave me my own copy of the Book of Mormon he said, with some embarrassment, that he'd told me things he's only told one of his three sons.

And I can't imagine what it was.

Maybe it was the 45-minute riff he did on the Holy Ghost. He talked a lot about math. He thought that I should understand that the Earth was precisely as old as Genesis proposes. He also urged me to consider other ways that numbers point to the divine.

"The Lord said all things will be reflected in me. All things reflected in me," he repeated. "How many apostles were there?"

"Twelve," I said.

"And how many players are there on an NBA team?"

He paused to let it sink in.

Despite such powerful testimony, he could tell at the end of the evening that I was far from persuaded and he was getting frustrated.

"You remind me of a friend of mine," he said, "a good friend who was just like you. One night he was drinking. He got up from his barstool and while he was crossing the street to his truck, he got hit by a car and it killed him."

I was struggling with the challenge of how to respond to such deep emotions when all I had really wanted was to check my e-mail. But finding myself without a suitable response, I shook his hand and went to bed.

That night I learned, among other things, why Bringham Young University has such a good basketball team. I discovered that the Book of Mormon makes a dandy theft deterrent when left on the dashboard of your vehicle. But the real lesson, I believe, was this:

If you're going to get drunk, don't park across the street from the bar.

37° 13' 48" N
113° 24' 43" W

Upper Quial

37° 13' 27" N
113° 24' 19" W

Parking

Take I-15 to exit #22. Turn onto the frontage road and drive south 3 mi, then turn right under the highway. Follow signs to the campground. Park in the day use area. Pay the $2 fee and hike about .6 mi to the first pool. Go left on ledges above it to reach the second pool.

0   .5   1 mile

Red Cliffs

You'll wear out several pairs of boots finding a slick rock canyon more sumptuous than this. The lower spot is really only a pot. The pool is trapezoid-shaped with lots of sand in the bottom. The fall and jump is only about six feet. It really needs a year or two of heavy snow runoff to rinse it clean. The better place is farther up where you find a little slot with a slide about seven feet high that spills into a rock walled pool that's 12 to 15 feet around. It's bounded by smooth, continuous red rock rising 50 feet. You gain the ledge above the pool by using some steps and an aid rope fastened above.

Expectation of privacy is zero. Gerald Grimmett has worked as the campground host since 1993. He describes Red Cliffs as an urban campground. On the Easter Holiday it can draw as many as 6,000. "We've got it pretty much under control now, but it used to be so rowdy that I wouldn't walk out the door without my pistol."

Average is three medical evacuations by helicopter per season, not all of them alcohol related either. The rocks produce a bumper crop of Moqui marbles which, when scattered on steep slick rock, means a quick trip to the bottom for anyone not extremely vigilant. A ranch upstream has water rights and if there is water flowing in the creek by Memorial Day, that's usually when they begin to exercise their right. So this is only an early, early season spot.

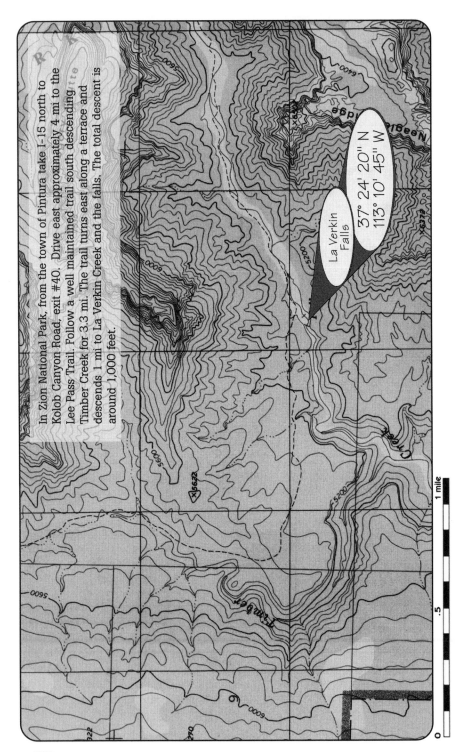

In Zion National Park, from the town of Pintura take I-15 north to Kolob Canyon Road, exit #40. Drive east approximately 4 mi to the Lee Pass Trail. Follow a well maintained trail south descending Timber Creek for 3.3 mi. The trail turns east along a terrace and descends 1 mi to La Verkin Creek and the falls. The total descent is around 1,000 feet.

La Verkin Falls

37° 24' 20" N
113° 10' 45" W

1 mile

.5

0

168

La Verkin Falls

Zion's back door. During the peak month, the park receives 12,000 visit *per day*, most of them in the southern portion. Only a tiny fraction, the *cognoccenti*, make it to the northwest corner and La Verkin Creek. There are several pools separated by a couple of hundred yards. The pattern is pretty consistent: Cascades and short falls nourish medium-sized pools all with little rock shoulders that are good to sit on or jump from. Really great backdrop, too. The stream is 200 or so yards from tall cliff walls, that although not absolutely sheer, rise an impressive 1,000 vertical feet.

The middle pool is the largest, about 25 feet in diameter. Not a big vertical description, though. Five chutes run 12 to 15 feet next to a deeply undercut rock wall. There's really no impound other than rocks and boulders. That limits depth and sand in the bottom can reduce depth further still. As a result, the sweet spot for jumps might be no more than six feet in diameter, so if you make a dive it better be a flat one.

Seating is tremendous at the middle fall. There is a deep alcove 50 feet above the second hole. It's flat, sandy and the ideal place to put down a picnic basket or stretch out for a nap. The lower hole also has some shade trees to escape from the relentless desert sun. Save some water and energy for the return trip. There's a one mile climb back out.

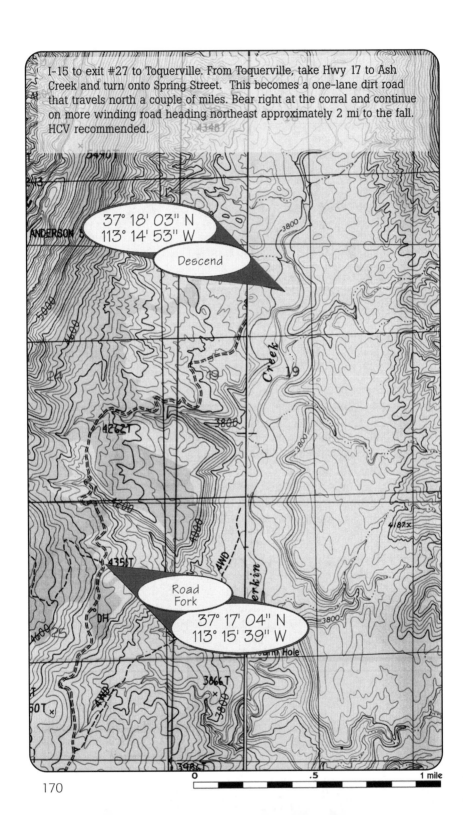

I-15 to exit #27 to Toquerville. From Toquerville, take Hwy 17 to Ash Creek and turn onto Spring Street. This becomes a one-lane dirt road that travels north a couple of miles. Bear right at the corral and continue on more winding road heading northeast approximately 2 mi to the fall. HCV recommended.

37° 18' 03" N
113° 14' 53" W

Descend

Road Fork

37° 17' 04" N
113° 15' 39" W

0 .5 1 mile

Three
Falls

It is to weep. The first fall is a cascade 15 to 20 feet high that stair-steps in six-foot increments, landing on a slab. No pool under it. The second is the swimming hole. It's about a ten foot plunge into a pool with the sides undercut by as much as six feet. The shape looks like a jug. There is a broad terrace to view the fall. Getting down to it requires some slipping and sliding on loose rock. Jumping is fun, but it takes two or three minutes to scramble back to the launch spot. Easily among the 20 best swimming holes in the southwest, but not a hiking destination. Not even a place to go without ear plugs on the weekend.

The bad news is that a dirt road goes up either side of the creek. You can even ride a motorbike across the lip of the fall. Beer bottles on the road and down by a really nasty fire pit. Bozos and yahoos abound. To wit: When I visited, a pickup driven by a young man with green hair was tailgating me and driving recklessly. I let him pass and three miles later I saw the truck hanging over the side of a 200 foot slope. A rescue attempt only sent it further down the slope.

"Same thing happened to me," one of the rescuers offered. "Three years ago. I was about half in the bag. I swerved to avoid some ATV and I went over the edge just like that."

All of which is to say, be really careful driving this road. Especially on weekends.

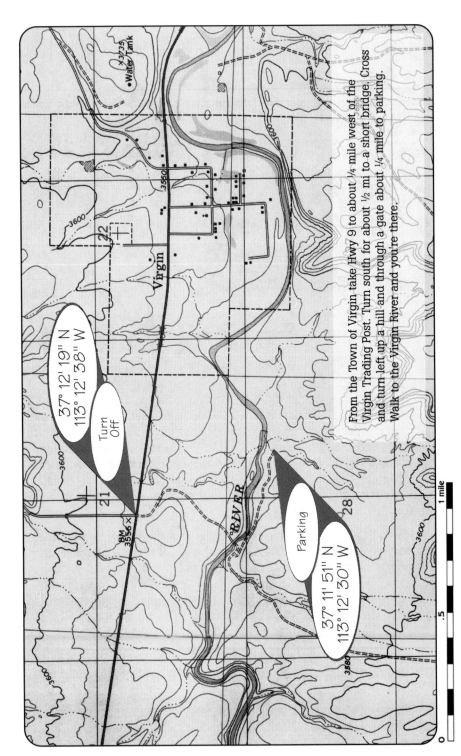

From the Town of Virgin take Hwy 9 to about ¼ mile west of the Virgin Trading Post. Turn south for about ½ mi to a short bridge. Cross and turn left up a hill and through a gate about ¼ mile to parking. Walk to the Virgin River and you're there.

37° 12' 19" N
113° 12' 38" W

Turn Off

37° 11' 51" N
113° 12' 30" W

Parking

Virgin

RIVER

Water Tank

1 mile

.5

0

172

Sheep Bridge

Swimming on a human scale. Here the Virgin River cuts through some limestone outside the village of Virgin and creates a small gorge that is unlike most places in the Southwest. Just about every other place in the region is epic—tall cliffs, long approaches, fast water. It's difficult to find a family swimming hole that the little dippers can make it to. Well, here it is.

The slot is little more than 100 yards long. The rock bench on the southern side of the river slopes down to meet the rapids at the top of the hole. At it's highest the ledge is less than 20 feet above the water. The ledges step down into what's usually deep water. Signs prohibit diving, though it still goes on. It's worth noting that it only takes one gully wash to change the bottom. What was safe to jump into last week might not be safe next week.

There are picnic tables, views of the sagebrush and even a couple of backyards. The approach is easy enough that you can bring the smallest members of the family. Heck, you can even bring grandma.

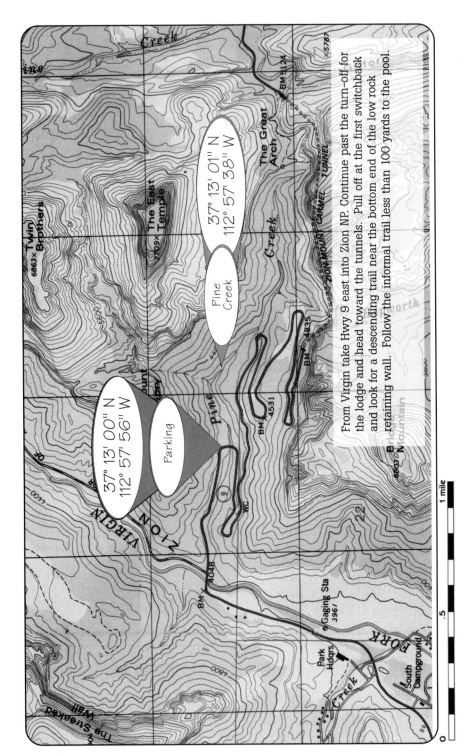

37° 13' 01" N
112° 57' 38" W

Pine
Creek

37° 13' 00" N
112° 57' 56" W

Parking

From Virgin take Hwy 9 east into Zion NP. Continue past the turn-off for the lodge and head toward the tunnels. Pull off at the first switchback and look for a descending trail near the bottom end of the low rock retaining wall. Follow the informal trail less than 100 yards to the pool.

0   .5   1 mile

174

Pine Creek

The fall is what most people see on lower Pine Creek. It's only about one-quarter mile from the road. There's a marginal pool at the bottom and the fall is worth a picture. The backdrop is out of this world. Mythic sandstone walls that people spend days climbing. What's more, visitorship is relatively light given the location and ease of access. But there's a better swimming hole about another quarter mile up Pine Creek.

It occurs where two big, blocky boulders fall flush against each other, creating the head wall. A similar collection of cabin-sized boulders completes the impound of an irregularly shaped pool 30 feet long at the broadest. Visitors regularly jump and dive from the boulders at the top of the pool. Heights are between five and seven feet. The bottom is sandy and it's entirely possible there will be too much sand and not enough water for jumping and diving.

In fact, it may not be deep enough to dive on Monday, then be clear and deep on Friday. Apparently it's difficult to guess whether a storm will fill a spot with wash or blow one clean down to the rock bottom. You just have to wade in and check it out.

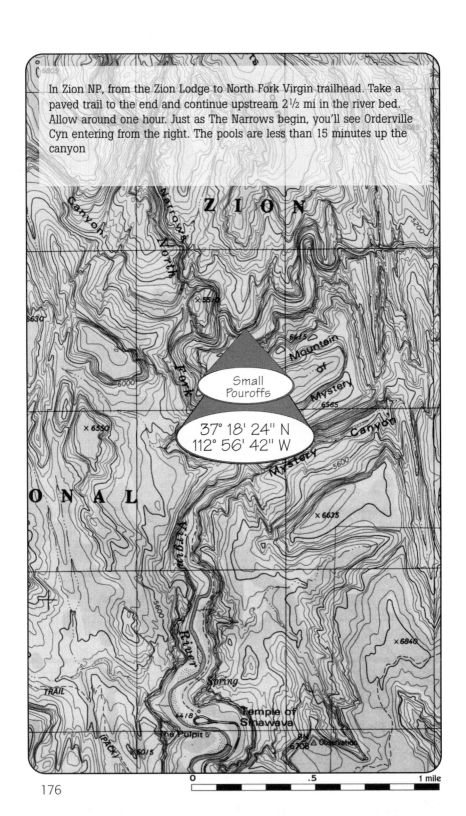

In Zion NP, from the Zion Lodge to North Fork Virgin trailhead. Take a paved trail to the end and continue upstream 2½ mi in the river bed. Allow around one hour. Just as The Narrows begin, you'll see Orderville Cyn entering from the right. The pools are less than 15 minutes up the canyon

Small Pouroffs

37° 18' 24" N
112° 56' 42" W

0   .5   1 mile

Orderville Falls

For all the attention that the Zion Narrows attracts, it doesn't offer much in the way of swimming holes. Water is cold since the deep canyon gets little sunlight. Nevertheless, consider a couple of pour-offs in Orderville Canyon where the early afternoon light is rich and the vegetation is gorgeous. Springs and seeps in the canyon walls support populations of western columbine, shooting star and pentstemon. They climb up the vertical rock like pastels hung on a museum wall.

The pools are less eye catching, more like tubs and buckets, really. The lower pools are within a couple of hundred yards from the mouth of the canyon. The middle pool is a small slot with a good looking fall. The pool at the bottom is little more than a few feet wide and chest deep. To get on the top, look for some tiny steps carved into the stone on the right.

The upper pool is more difficult. You have to swim through a brief slot or complete a scramble with a couple of tricky steps and a potentially injurious fall. The pool is no more than six feet deep, not user friendly and difficult to reach. The best feature is a small alcove/pothole carved into the canyon wall on the left about twelve vertical feet above the channel. The floor is a flat, level patch of sand just big enough for a pair of reclining bodies to stretch out in the shade and admire the verdant walls.

Wheel
Barrow

37° 02' 38" N
112° 57' 21" W

Parking

37° 02' 12" N
112° 57' 09" W

37° 00' 53" N
112° 57' 41" W

Bear
Right

From Hurricane take Hwy 59 south approximately 22 mi to Hildale. Turn
left onto Utah St and drive 2 mi east, then follow the road as it turns
north about ¼ mi and then becomes dirt. After 600 yds, a jeep trail
forks right. (If you get to the park, you went too far.) Drive just under 2
mi to the reservoir and park

0   .5   1 mile

Water Canyon

The farthest thing from a clothing optional swimming hole you could imagine. This is well off the tourist trail. Water Canyon is the local swimming hole for Hilldale, an isolated community on the Utah-Arizona border. Isolated, but well known. It's situated at the bottom of a little canyon called Short Creek. Locals, a rustic group, pronounce it, "cshaort crick" and it has become shorthand for the 10,000 or so polygamists who live here. They're called "Crickers."

The women wear dresses patterned after 19th Century pioneer garb. Both sexes wear long underwear day and night, year round as a symbol of their covenant with God. Long sleeves are the rule and men working in the fields will not even roll up their cuffs on the hottest day of summer for fear of being considered immodest. It's all very odd, but if you visit please exercise restraint in your bathing attire to avoid scandalizing the populace.

These are small pools. The main one is immediately below a tiny natural arch. There is also a pretty little set of falls above. Historically these pools have been deeper, but when reviewed it was hardly deep enough for a jump off a small rock. Local kids have attempted to raise the level by piling rocks and even pieces of plywood and plastic at the bottom. It looks a little bit ugly. They call it "wheel barrow" after one that was left there as part of the effort to build an impound.

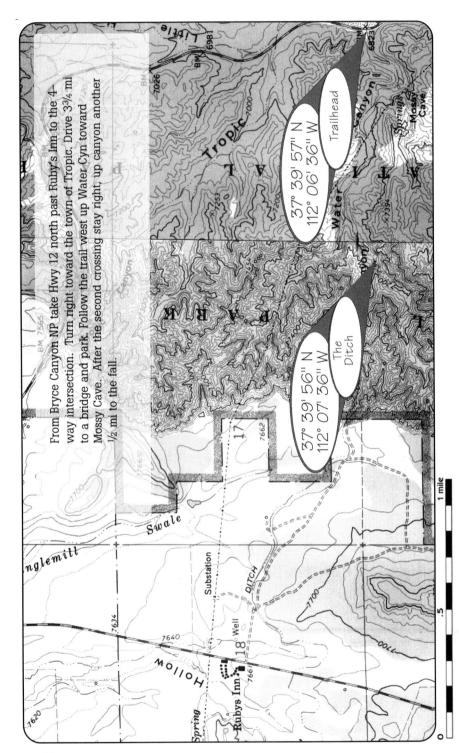

From Bryce Canyon NP take Hwy 12 north past Ruby's Inn to the 4-way intersection. Turn right toward the town of Tropic. Drive 3¾ mi to a bridge and park. Follow the trail west up Water Cyn toward Mossy Cave. After the second crossing stay right up canyon another ½ mi to the fall.

37° 39' 57" N
112° 06' 36" W
Trailhead

37° 39' 56" N
112° 07' 36" W
The Ditch

.5   1 mile

Tropic Ditch

Call this the law of unintended consequences. Or how Mormon pioneers attracted Frenchmen in Speedos.

Nineteenth Century settlers around the town of Tropic got thirsty. They peeled off a piece of the Sevier River and sent it down an otherwise dry canyon toward their town. Soon the alfalfa was thick and the cows were fat.

Now fast forward 100 years.

Places like Bryce Canyon and Zion have become vacation desti-nations for thousands of people, among them a high proportion of Euro's fascinated by the vastness and colors of south Utah. Here, where an exotic plume of water companions with the famed Pink Cliffs, you get French people hiking in teeny, tiny swim suits.

The Ditch is a visual attraction apart from the Frogs in Spandex. The diversion runs a mostly flat course through the Pink Cliffs until is gets to a shelf about 15 feet high. It a beautiful plunge, but the pool at the bottom is barely deep enough to be reviewed here. The rock type in Bryce is just too brittle to make a nice deep hole. It seems that whatever the water removes is back filled by more crumbled rock.

Moab, Escalante & the Canyonlands

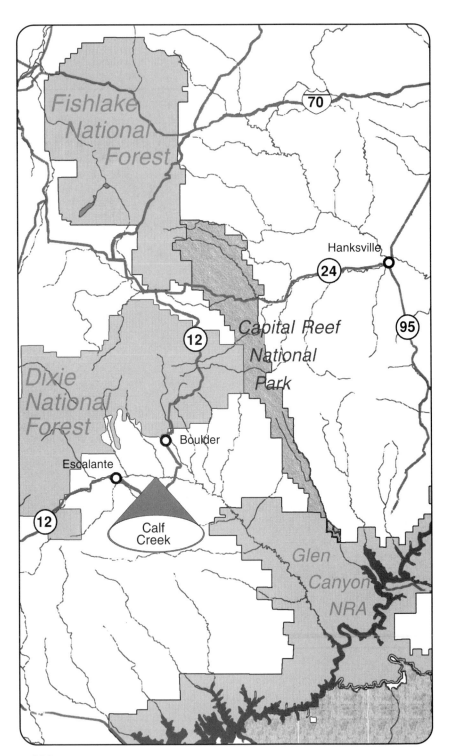

Fishlake
National
Forest

Dixie
National
Forest

Capital Reef
National
Park

Glen
Canyon
NRA

Hanksville

Boulder

Escalante

Calf
Creek

70

24

95

12

12

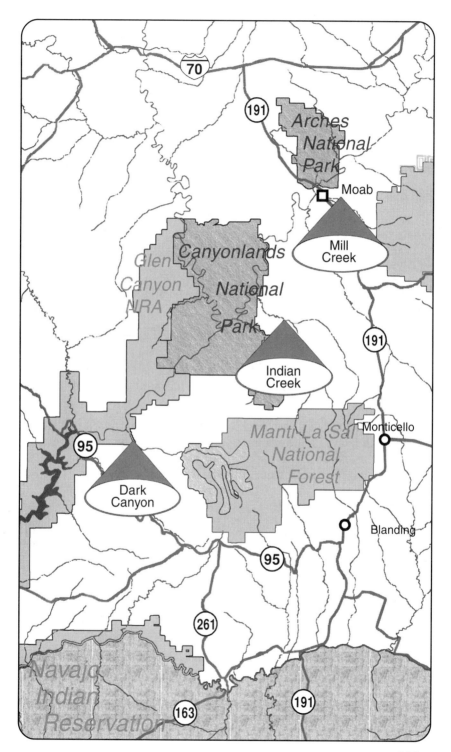

Arches
National
Park

Moab

Mill
Creek

Glen Canyonlands
Canyon National
NRA Park

Indian
Creek

Manti La Sal
National
Forest

Monticello

Dark
Canyon

Blanding

Navajo
Indian
Reservation

70

191

191

95

95

261

163

191

185

Hymn to the Metatarsals

In Moab people aren't strangers for very long. Here, people study centuries-old petroglyphs in the surrounding canyons for modern meaning . After the second cup of chai, a resident might recount a period during the 70s when they ate psychedelic mushrooms daily. Outside a scruffy man pedals a homemade bike around town muttering, "Mexicans eat free. Mexicans eat free."

Whether or not that's true, most Utah in towns discourage men like him. In Moab, they blend in.

A short walk from the tourist galleries and bike shops is Michael Cree's front door. Taped to it is picture of Sai Baba and next to the bagvadita is a cardboard sign that says, "Popcorn."

"That's because I'm the Popcorn Jellybean," Cree said. "Popcorn, because I'm from Iowa. And the Jellybean is because the world is like a jellybean."

He explained, but I didn't follow. So he defended the name choice with an anecdote.

"One day I saw a guy dressed in a dashiki. When I asked his name, he said Jellybean Popcorn. Now what are the odds of that?"

I met Michael at the café where his girlfriend works. I was limping slightly from an inflamed tendon in my foot, and since everyone in Moab is either a massage therapist or living with one, I thought I might get some free advice along with my latte. But in the way a cafe conversation skips around, we quickly began exchanging Alaska stories and, since he lived there for ten years, his were naturally better than mine.

The Alaska residence was part of 25 years spent along the Pacific Rim, where he's been compiling a set of spiritual beliefs and exercising vigorously.

"In Maui I was using my in-line skates a lot and I had a titanium road bike. Skulling, too. Plus, I've skipped rope in Fiji, New Zealand, Australia *and* Indonesia."

As a collegiate, he wrestled for the University of Iowa. More than 30 years later, he's a freelance landscaper who admits he made a bad career move by leaving the lush Pacific Islands for the Utah desert.

But at 52, he still has legs like a racehorse, the flexibility of a teenager and a kid's enthusiasm for metaphysical topics. While boiling noodles and steaming greens for supper, he explained a few things.

"We're just spirits occupying this dimension," he said. "We're capable of traveling in so many different planes, so many different places. A friend of mine from Moab was out for ten days over around Paradox in Colorado. He shot a rabbit for supper and while he was cooking it he heard this voice behind him ask, 'You going to share that rabbit?'

"It was Black Crow, the last of the peaceful chiefs. His spirit materialized and for three days, the two of them walked all through those mountains together."

"My foot," I said.

"What?"

"My foot. What do you think I should do about this sore foot?"

He demonstrated, among other things, a yoga position. I think it was called the "Reclining Buddha," or something. He extended himself on the floor with his head propped on his elbow. I looked at him stretched there and told him that back home we call that "Watching Television."

It was unfair, but earlier he told me that I wasn't the sort of person a UFO would abduct, and I guess I was feeling a little hurt. Nevertheless, he sent me off with some photocopied chants, a story about angels downloaded from the Internet and a primer on aura repair.

Apparently I didn't follow the instructions because a couple of days later my foot was hurting again when I came up behind a group of six urban women hiking toward the same swimming hole I was visiting. The tall pretty one said that she was a Methodist minister and a physical therapist. The group was visiting the fall to conduct a baptism.

There was some milling about before the ceremony, then a brief commotion. One of the women was trying to feed a piece of dried fruit to a snake.

I wanted to stay and explore this strange metaphor, and maybe get some therapy tips for the foot. But it was starting to rain, so I gimped back down the trail. And what the hell? I knew I would never get comprable quotes from a Methodist.

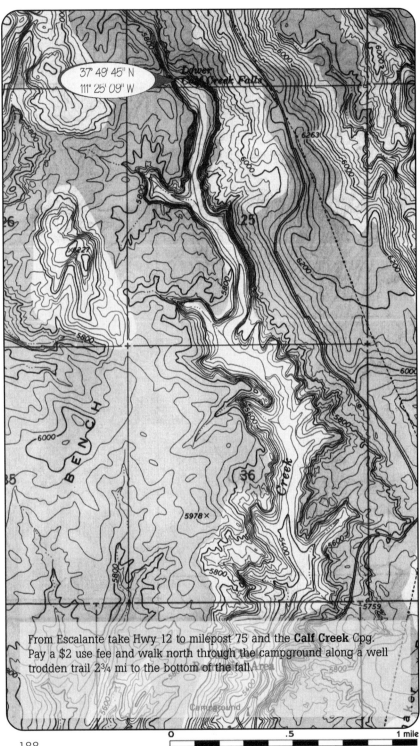

37° 49' 45" N
111° 25' 09" W

Lower
Calf Creek Falls

6263

5227

BENCH

6000

5978 ×

5759

From Escalante take Hwy 12 to milepost 75 and the **Calf Creek** Cpg.
Pay a $2 use fee and walk north through the campground along a well
trodden trail 2¾ mi to the bottom of the fall.

Campground

0   .5   1 mile

Lower Calf Creek

The walls at the head of the canyon are at least 150 feet high, some more than 200 feet tall – twice as tall as the canyon floor is wide. It looks like a glacial cirque. The fall comes down in two jumps, 126 total feet. The top part of the cascade is inaccessible. The bottom flume lands on steep shoulder of rock, then discharges into a broad, sandy pool that's fan shaped and shallow throughout until you get to within 10 feet of the plunge itself. It's a little uncomfortable in the deep part because water will be pelting you at fairly high velocity.

The beach is brilliant. It's a crescent 15 feet wide that surrounds the waterline. It then slopes gently upward to a point about 45 feet back from the water and disappears into mixed vegetation and shady alders. Looks like the lagoon on Gilligan's Island. Adding to the tropical appearance is a belt of vegetation climbing up the wall where a host of other water-loving species make a living in the cool, damp box canyon.

After water from Calf Creek and the Escalante River travel under the bridge on Hwy 12, it belongs to water districts in Southern California. Residents complain that the town of Escalante had to drill a well 3,200 feet deep just to reach a source of poor quality water.

Lower Calf Creek

Upper Calf Creek

It's the same basic design as Lower Calf Creek, only the surrounding walls are not as high. The fall is 87 feet high. Just to the left of the fall a steep rock ramp runs 35 feet, all of it covered with slimy, lower plant life. This greases the surface well enough to use it for a slide, as demonstrated by visiting Boy Scout troops. Choose the descent carefully, though. God only gave you one tailbone.

The fall has carved a bell-shaped space out of the sandstone and created a cool, humid place inside the bowl that supports a succulent grasses that literally grow up the wall. Wild roses complete the effect of a soft nursery of green surrounded by sun and sandstone. The pool is 10 feet deep and about 60 feet in diameter, but since this is basically a sand and mud impound with lots of surrounding vegetation, there is no good place to sit. It's much warmer early in the season than at Lower Calf Creek Fall. By late June, it's apt to become a muddy hole. The spur trail is well marked and less than ¼ mile long. Please stay on the trail and don't wander or you risk damaging the fragile riparian fringe like the wild roses.

This is the same trailhead as Top Calf. Only difference is that to reach Top Calf you pass the descending spur and continue about 200 feet up the trail.

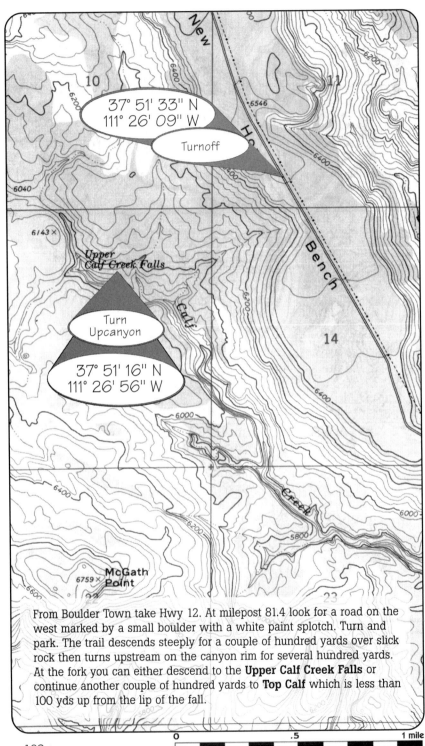

37° 51' 33" N
111° 26' 09" W

Turnoff

Upper
Calf Creek Falls

Turn
Upcanyon

37° 51' 16" N
111° 26' 56" W

From Boulder Town take Hwy 12. At milepost 81.4 look for a road on the west marked by a small boulder with a white paint splotch. Turn and park. The trail descends steeply for a couple of hundred yards over slick rock then turns upstream on the canyon rim for several hundred yards. At the fork you can either descend to the **Upper Calf Creek Falls** or continue another couple of hundred yards to **Top Calf** which is less than 100 yds up from the lip of the fall.

0   .5   1 mile

Top
Calf

Great training ground for the little dippers. This is a dandy hole with a deep rock bottom and a jumping ledge around 12-feet high. The impound is 40 feet wide and surrounded on about 200 degrees by a rock wall of exfoliating slabs. The tank is around 10 feet deep. The jump is on the left as you face upstream. After splashdown, swim across to the left side to exit and scramble back to the top.

At the top of the fall, water rolls in a thin veneer over smooth rock. Shade comes from a couple of small cottonwoods you can duck into about 50 feet above the hole. Other than that, seating is limited. Consider bringing something to relax on. But less than 100 yards downstream, at the lip of the big fall, there's enough seating for a whole classroom. It's set at a smooth, gentle angle that's more comfortable than anything you'll find at the Hilton.

The trip is a little more than one mile. The trail is well marked and negotiable in sneakers. You might make the little ones jog all the way back to wear them out enough to allow mom and dad a moment alone in the evening.

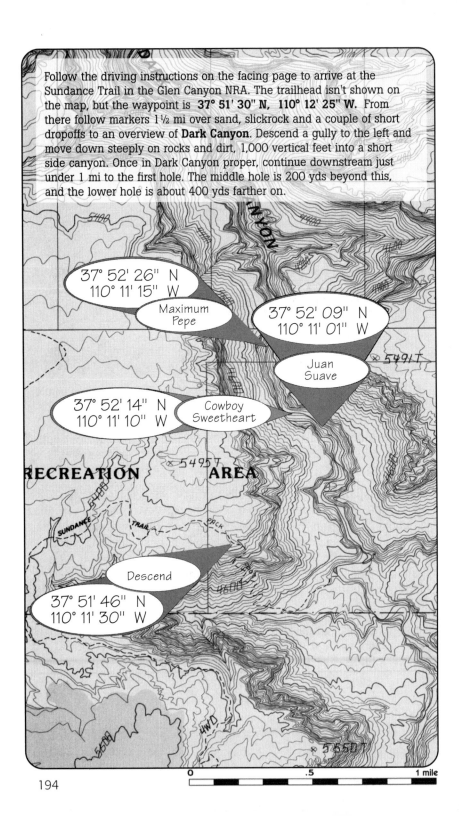

Follow the driving instructions on the facing page to arrive at the Sundance Trail in the Glen Canyon NRA. The trailhead isn't shown on the map, but the waypoint is **37° 51' 30" N, 110° 12' 25" W.** From there follow markers 1½ mi over sand, slickrock and a couple of short dropoffs to an overview of **Dark Canyon**. Descend a gully to the left and move down steeply on rocks and dirt, 1,000 vertical feet into a short side canyon. Once in Dark Canyon proper, continue downstream just under 1 mi to the first hole. The middle hole is 200 yds beyond this, and the lower hole is about 400 yds farther on.

37° 52' 26" N
110° 11' 15" W

Maximum
Pepe

37° 52' 09" N
110° 11' 01" W

Juan
Suave

37° 52' 14" N
110° 11' 10" W

Cowboy
Sweetheart

RECREATION   AREA

× 5495T

SUNDANCE   TRAIL

Descend

37° 51' 46" N
110° 11' 30" W

0   .5   1 mile

Juan Suave

A green crescent inset in red stone. Water is forced into a tiny bend by a sweet sunning rock. Ledges step up on the right, (as you face up canyon) and there's a cobble and sand embankment on the left. Canyon walls are as high as 400 feet above the pool. Very impressive, but despite this, there are no good jumps. The best it can offer are limestone ledges about two feet high. The pool's on the smallish side, although the ledges give it depth of seven feet or so. The best entry is from the sunning rock. It's about 15 feet in circumference, tilted at a low angle and set smack in the apex of the pool. Stand up, walk to the edge and tip over into cool, cool water.

The most difficult thing is finding the trailhead among the many miles of dirt road. There are a couple of directions to approach from. I prefer starting at the junction of Hite Marina Road and State Route 95. Drive east one quarter mile to County Road 208A (aka Road 632), a graded dirt road that's suitable for HCV vehicles. Take 208A southeast for about 7½ miles to 209A. Continue southeast one mile on 209A, then turn northeast (still on 209A) approximately 2.5 miles to a butte and prominent spire named Squaw & Papoose Rock. If you don't have 4WD, you may park here and hike one mile over the mesa heading 23 degrees to intersect the Sundance Trail.

Alternately, you can follow the road from Pappose Rock as it curves southeast and reaches a 4WD road that runs three miles north to the trailhead.

Dark Canyon

Cowboy Sweetheart

I love this place. It exemplifies the color combination of Southwest swimming holes: Red rock, green water and blue sky. This water is a gorgeous emerald color, deep and clear. It's a little slot about 30 feet long and perfectly framed top to bottom. Not any jumping, but you might be able to get six feet off one of the terraces on the right.

Like so many other nicely shaped holes, this one occurs where the rock slabs are aligned on the same plane as the water flow. Thus, the water acts to erode a smooth, homogenous surface and creates a uniform pool instead of working across the grain of the rockbed, breaking off chunks that produce boulder clutter.

The approach is on ledges 35 to 40 vertical feet above the creek, but cairns let you know where to scramble down to the water. Tons of comfy places to sit once there, and probably some company. Dark Canyon gets visited. Expect as many as five cars on a weekend. However, the steep descent keeps use fairly light. Maybe only a couple of people get to this pool.

Dark Canyon

Maximum Pepe

Largest of the three Dark Canyon swimming holes. This one is in a slot with vertical sides on the left as you look upstream and terraces on the right about 10 feet above water. A chute about 25 feet long supplies the hole, however ridges in the rock make what might otherwise be a great water slide into little more than a pretty feature.

An excellent swimming hole, but it loses points for lack of seating and a difficult entry and exit. There's a little pad of rock in the pool on the right, 'bout the size of a park bench. No room to stretch out, though. As for hauling out of the water, sides are vertical and crumbling. The best advice is to exit using the ledges next to the chute on the left.

The trip down into the canyon is a good geological resume. At the top, the light colored formation streaked with black desert varnish is Cedar Mesa sandstone. Below that are Cutler beds, red and white stone comprised of both limestone and sandstone. The inner core of the canyon is Hermosa formation, gray limestone, sandstone and shale. Look for some interesting inclusions of dark, blood-red chert, too.

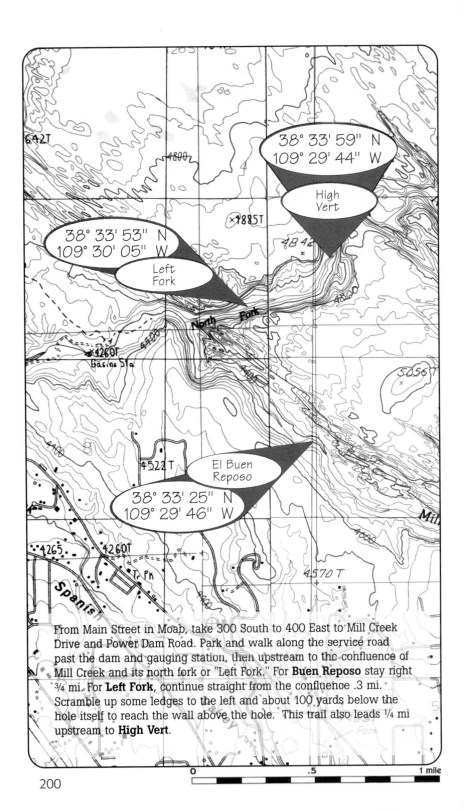

38° 33' 59" N
109° 29' 44" W

High
Vert

38° 33' 53" N
109° 30' 05" W

Left
Fork

El Buen
Reposo

38° 33' 25" N
109° 29' 46" W

From Main Street in Moab, take 300 South to 400 East to Mill Creek
Drive and Power Dam Road. Park and walk along the service road
past the dam and gauging station, then upstream to the confluence of
Mill Creek and its north fork or "Left Fork." For **Buen Reposo** stay right
¾ mi. For **Left Fork**, continue straight from the confluence .3 mi.
Scramble up some ledges to the left and about 100 yards below the
hole itself to reach the wall above the hole. This trail also leads ¼ mi
upstream to **High Vert**.

0   .5   1 mile

El Buen Reposo

A modest pool that's outshone by the canyon around it. Here, about one mile above the trailhead, the canyon opens up to grassy benches, wildflowers and juniper. The best part is the backdrop. A set of several rock fins 200 feet tall or more stand behind it and dominate the scene.

The pool itself pales by comparison. It's maybe seven feet deep and only three feet wide. The container is formed by short walls that provide a nice place to dangle your legs, but that's about it. The water makes an attractive run into the pool, spilling through a little slot and a couple of cascades before emptying into a half pipe that's unfortunately too small for a water slide, plus it discharges directly into the left wall. Good sunning slabs, but not lots of accompanying shade other than a couple of scrubby junipers. The trail is so soft and well-trodden that you can travel bare foot. Sandals are recommended, though. A couple of crossings might be ankle deep.

Lots of tourists. There's even a bird in the canyon whose song sounds remarkably like a Motorola.

Left Fork

Everybody knows about Left Fork and there's a reason: The hole is bodacious. It's a wedge-shaped slice of heaven that measures 40 feet wide or more. Most important are big headwalls on both sides of the fall. The right wall is around 20-feet tall. The left is more than 30 feet. Both are popular jumping spots. The sides are steeply undercut and the landing is 8-feet deep or more. There are potential diving hazards, however. Consequently, the sweet spot under both jumps is about 4-5 feet wide, so some judgement is required before launching.

You need to use some judgement even to enter this canyon. Exercising outdoor ethics is paramount here.

"People who come and visit, remember you are just one of thousands," says Kara Dohrenwend of the Mill Creek Partnership. They're the ones who pick up the trash left by bozos and blockheads as well as replanting the vegetation that they trample. The partnership budgeted $50,000 for conservation and restoration of the canyon for one year alone.

"It seems like a minor thing to walk off the trail to check out a cool plant or a cave. Well in a few weeks that path is going to become a three feet wide. It takes lots of time and money for the people who live here to restore it."

High Vert

Attractively cross-bedded stone below, with pale pink walls towering 600 feet above. A pool about 45 feet on the long side is fed by a low cascade that, during perfect conditions, rolls softly into the deep end of the pool. Not diving deep, though. There's nothing to jump from and the sandy bottom limits depth. Seating is on a thin strip of sand and cobble at the bottom of the pool.

The water eventually reaches Power Dam, a small hole at the end of the road heading up Mill Creek Canyon. Power Dam is a rowdy spot that produces it's share of injuries. One notable story involves Moab cop Greg Neilson. He volunteered and trained for the search and rescue team. On his first day he got a call for a rescue at Power Dam where he found his brother lying at the bottom with a broken neck. Neilson and the others bundled his brother onto a backboard, evacuated and transported him to the hospital where he made a full recovery.

"One of those television shows, the ones that have police chases and rescues was interested in it," he said, "but that's about all. Nothing ever came of it."

The problem was not lack of drama, just no good video.

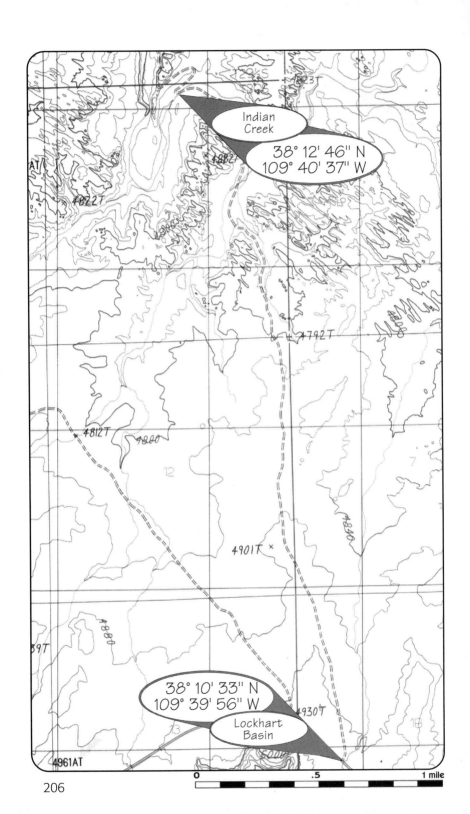

Indian
Creek

38° 12' 46" N
109° 40' 37" W

4882T

4822T

4792T

4812T

4800

12

4901T ×

4880

39T

38° 10' 33" N
109° 39' 56" W

4930T

Lockhart
Basin

4961AT

0   .5   1 mile

Indian Creek

A pretty little bowl, about 30 feet wide and 20 feet deep. A band of limestone creates a hole with steep sides, but a shallow bottom. There's an adjacent ledge about eight feet above the pool. The pool is good during low water for kids even though the steep sides mean it takes a couple of minutes to get all the way back to the car on the road above.

Don't be surprised to find some Dutch or French tourists parked next to you. This part of the Southwest is a popular destination for European tourists. "They're fascinated by the emptiness of it, said Tracey Napoleone, who along with her husband runs The Outpost, a general store on the road to Indian Creek.

It's not a hiking destination, though. Indian Creek isn't in the Canyonlands National Park; it's in the Canyon Rims Recreation Area. The difference is that you're permitted to drive a four-wheeler directly to the creek.

From Moab, take Hwy 191 south 40 mi to Road 221. Go 13½ mi southwest toward Canyonlands NP and Newspaper Rock. At Newspaper Rock the road bends northwest 20 mi to Lockhart Basin Rd. (Road #122) Drive north on Lockhart Basin 3¼ miles to the crossing and park. High-clearance vehicle is recommended for Lockhart Basin, but not normally required.

Why Bother

Emerald Pools

Escalante. Over visited.

Freemont Falls

Pretty. And good jumping, too. But heavily visited as it's right next to a road in Capitol Reef National Park .

Negro Bill

Sand, rock and lots of dead vegetation due to a robust population of beavers. The oversized rodents have killed at least half a dozen mature cottonwoods and generally mucked up what was a marginal swimming stream at best.

Ken's Lake

A diversion of Mill Creek and a big, powerful waterfall. But it isn't natural, you can drive up to it, plus there's not much of a pool at the bottom.

Kane Creek

The creek is paralleled by an four-wheel drive road and who wants to share a swimming hole with a Suzuki?

256 pages
Retail Price: $18.95
Author: Pancho Doll
ISBN **0-9657686-5-6**
Christmas 2005

Go figure. After suffering rain and fog all winter, when the sun comes out in summer, the first thing people in Oregon and Washinton want to do is get wet. ***Northwestern Swimming Holes*** covers the Cascade Mountains, south past Seattle to Portland. The rest of Oregon occupies the middle of the book with coverage extending to the California Redwoods.

312 pages
Retail Price: $18.95
Author: Pancho Doll
ISBN **0-96576861-9**

A guide to remote creeks and rivers from the
Virginias through Pennsylvania, New York and New
England. *Northeastern Swimming Holes* includes
photos of each destination as well as topographic maps
with GPS waypoints. More than 300 entries.

Registered users can print individual maps from the
website, then tuck it in a pocket. That way they don't
carry an entire book when they only need one page.

256 pages
Retail Price: $18.95
Author: Pancho Doll
ISBN **0-96576864-3**

California Splash finds the best water in the
Golden State. Covering everything from the northern
redwoods to the southern deserts, it features 105 trips
ranging from child friendly to technical approaches with
rope. Secluded waterfalls, remote two-person tubs, and
hidden pools. Clothing optional spots are noted. Icons
tell dog owners if four-legged hikers are appropriate,
and families with small children can tell at a glance if
the hike is a good one for the little dippers.

256 pages
Retail Price: $18.95
Author: Pancho Doll
ISBN **0-9657686-3-5**
Spring 2005

Nowhere is the culture of the dip deeper than in the southeast. During summer months, employers rate the river as the third-leading cause of workplace absentee-ism. ***Southeastern Swimming Holes*** covers the West Virginia mountains, through highland rivers of North Carolina to the headwaters of North Georgia. It contains more than 350 places to get wet south of the Mason-Dixon Line.

MORNING EDITION

The host of National Public Radio's morning news program asked the author how he finds the places featured in his books. The answer is sometimes luck, the bad kind:

"My brakes failed in the Tennessee mountains. I managed to coast to a little garage where the man fixed the leak and told me about a swimming hole I would not have found otherwise.

"I'm hoping for clutch trouble in North Carolina."

The West's leading lifestyle magazine ran a one-page story in the front of its *Sunset* May 2004 issue. The magazine's broad distribution and presence at supermarket checkout stands throughout the state introduced people to the book that looks up every canyon and to the author's motto: "I get lost so you don't have to."

Esquire The magazine devoted to "Man At His Best" inked the Day Trips with a Splash series for three summers running. It proclaimed Doll a *cult figure,* and although he admits there's no factual basis for the claim, he says that it does look good on a résumé.

ABC's Brian Rooney spent two days with the author, contrasting wilderness swimming holes with the cut and cast water  parks most people associate with wet, summer fun. The segment which ran July 2004 on World News Tonight with Peter Jennings marked the first time that the Emmy Award winning reporter took off his shirt for a story.

The June '03 issue profiled author Pancho Doll along with 15 of his favorite spots nationwide. The eight-page story talks about the difficulty of retaining a normal life and relationships while annually traveling a distance equal to circumnavigating the equator.

"At a party I told some friends that I thought of myself as the wind. My girlfriend dug an elbow into my side and asked, 'If you're the wind, then whose crap is that on my back porch?' "

The author appeared on NBC's Today Show speaking live, via satellite from the Blue Ridge Mountains. After talking about the outdoor life and showing a collection of photos, Doll demonstrated what's got to be the best job commute in America, leaping from an adjoining rock ledge into the river to conclude the Memorial Day broadcast.

TODAY